MR. NARY

The Story of How Grady Thoms Got Published

MR. NARY

The Story of How Grady Thoms Got Published

ROO CARMICHAEL

RCPress

Mr. Nary
The Story of How Grady Thoms Got Published
© 2014 by Roo Carmichael
roocarmichael.com

Published by RCPress,
an imprint of Deep River Books
PO Box 310
Sisters, OR 97759

ISBN – 13: 9781940269191
ISBN – 10: 1940269199

Library of Congress: 2014934975

Printed in the USA

Cover design by Connie Gabbert

December

To: Bill Williams
From: Grady Thoms
Subject: Book Idea

Hi Bill, my name is Grady Thoms (the "h" is silent). Your book, *The Missionary*, was recommended by my cousin Jesse, who shares my interest in political foreign thrillers. I was very impressed and read it in four days. I really identified with your main character, David Eller, whose good intentions ended up advancing Communism (the bad kind) in Venezuala. Your book serves as a good reminder that we should all do a little more research on the beatnik communes or radical militia groups we plan to join—even the ones with killer mission statements. Before you know it, you're part of a group that hates farmers and won't eat butter. And at night you're sleeping in a canoe with two other dudes wondering if this movement is really contributing to society.

Anyway, you will be happy to know that you have inspired me to write my own novel. I would like to write something important and meaningful, like my friend Chet who wrote the Wikipedia pages for Steer Wrestling and Axe Body Wash. I have come up with a few ideas. They are not quite at the level of *The Missionary* but let me know what you think.

My first idea is about a guy named Travis who wishes he could have a bigger house, a better job, and more worldly possessions. He is a religious man and attends church, but the fast-paced lifestyle of Salt Lake City gets the best of him. He finds himself in trouble with the government when he starts to print counterfeit money to fit the lifestyle he envisions to start soon. However, he is so bad at counterfeiting that the money doesn't look real and the government has no case against him. He dodged a bullet, phew. But not so fast! As it turns out, the counterfeit money looks a lot like Canadian money, and the Royal Mounties are ready to pounce on him if he ever decides to enter Canada (I did research in Canada for this part). Travis never goes to Canada, but he does come close when he visits a cousin in Michigan. He is sad for his loss to never vacation in Canada, but he must accept those consequences. Travis wishes he would have never counterfeited and he wishes he would have never wanted more possessions. I call this book *The Wishionary*.

My second book idea is a cautionary tale for YA (young adults) dealing with family situations. It's about a lady who is so excited about her wedding, but one problem—she's not engaged to anybody! She's not even dating, but that doesn't stop her from planning a beautiful Renaissance wedding. For most of the book, we follow her daily adventures when she starts to suspect her sister and dad of trying to sabotage her big day. She grows more suspicious of her family and friends and believes they are secretly keeping her from meeting a man. In the end, she does not get married and commits suicide in her wedding dress. I call this book *The Suspicionary.*

My last book idea is probably the best and it really gets the blood flowing. It's about a private eye named Chuck Nary who must travel to Bolivia during a time when US–Bolivian relations are mediocre at best. He has a mission to find a couple who disappeared while their cruise ship was docked at a Bolivian port. They were just tourists. Who would want to kidnap them, right? Chuck Nary travels to Bolivia, and after a few days, realizes Bolivia is a landlocked country with no port. It was a trap! No couple was actually kidnapped. I'm not going to give away any more secrets, but a few ideas I have include dangerous documents, poison, llama chases, hidden staircases, really long stakeouts, and a love-starved orphanage mother of nine. I call this book *Mister Nary.*

Thanks,

Grady

- - - - - - - - - - - - - - - - - - -

To: Grady Thoms
From: Bill Williams
Re: Book Idea

Grady, please send us your resume, including your name, address, and phone number. We need this information before we can consider any query. Thank you,
Bill Williams Acquisitions and Press

- - - - - - - - - - - - - - - - - - -

To: Bill Williams
From: Grady Thoms
Re: Book Idea

Bill, thanks for the quick response. For the record, I am not a query and am not sure what gave you that impression. I don't even know who they are but I probably do not agree with their lifestyle.

Just so you know, I am hesitant to give up my personal information. It's not that I don't trust you or BWA. I just don't want my information floating in cyberspace at random. I receive way too much junk mail as it is. Yesterday I received an issue of *Turkish Delight,* a mail-order bride catalog from Turkey. How do these people get my address? Yes, a couple of the girls were attractive, but I want to find my wife the traditional way, like at the roller rink or at a town hall meeting. I am in no way saying you give out stuff to the Turkish mail-order bride people, but they will do anything to get information.

I have sent my book ideas to you, Random House, Simon & Schuster, Doubleday, and Armageddon Books. So far, you are the only one to respond.

Thanks,
Grady

- - - - - - - - - - - - - - - - - - - -

To: Bill Williams
From: Grady Thoms
Subject: Getting Started

Bill, I'm really working hard on my novel now. I'm going with the idea of the private eye Chuck Nary flying to Bolivia to save the kidnapped tourists. Do you think I need to go to Bolivia to do research for this? Tickets are really expensive. I went to the library and read parts of Rick Steebes traveling guide on Bolivia, so I feel up to speed. Did you know that soybeans are a major cash crop? I will definitely work that in.

What else do I need to do to get ready for this book?
Thanks,
Grady

To: Grady Thoms
From: Bill Williams
Re: Getting Started

Grady, I am afraid I do not have much time to help you with your new venture. While I respect and admire those with the courage to explore fresh literary pursuits, I will not be able to offer much advice and coaching due to other commitments.

I suggest you read some books about writing good fiction. A couple I can recommend are *How to Write a Damn Good Novel: A Step-by-Step No Nonsense Guide to Dramatic Storytelling* by James N. Frey and *On Writing Well* by William Zinsser (a little dated but good).

After you have a handle on the basics of writing fiction, you will need to map out an outline of the novel and create character profiles for all the major players. I hope this helps. Good luck.

Regards,

Bill

- - - - - - - - - - - - - - - - - - -

To: Bill Williams
From: Grady Thoms
Subject: Opening Lines

Bill, I've heard that opening lines are critical when writing fiction. Is this correct? I want to suck the reader in right away. They should be standing in Powell's Books or Barnsin Nobles, well into chapter 2, when they suddenly realize they're late to pick up their child from day care. That's how intense I want the first paragraph to be. I have a couple possibilities. Maybe you could help me choose.

> *It was 4:09 a.m. when Chuck Nary opened his eyes to feel the cold muzzle of steel pressed against his temple. He knew it could be any one of a dozen people who wanted him dead. If it was the Big Samoan or one of Gordon's hired goons, he'd be in hell by now. Nary closed his eyes to think. It could only be one of two people, both women; one spoiled, one spurned.*

Or do you like this one better:

After trudging through the wet wilderness for the better part of two days, the trained assassins finally had the cabin in sight. Although they did not know much about their intended target, Mr. Nary, he was not to be taken lightly. Rumor had it that he was the only one to survive the grisly roller coaster accident at the Barterville County Fair last summer.

Either one of these paragraphs can work for the first chapter, which is halfway written. I just might have to change a few things around for continuity. Both are pretty intense and will get almost anyone jazzed to read on. Let me know what you think.

Thanks,

Grady

- - - - - - - - - - - - - - - - - - - -

To: Grady Thoms
From: Bill Williams
Re: Opening Lines

Grady, thorough character profiles should be done before you start writing. For each main character, you need to create a history. What are their traits? Include family life. Are they married? Do they have children? Where do they work? It is very important you do this before you begin.

As I mentioned before, I really don't have time to act as editor for you at this stage of your learning curve. I think you need to practice writing fiction for a while and then maybe we can review your work down the road.

Regards,

Bill

- - - - - - - - - - - - - - - - - - - -

To: Bill Williams
From: Grady Thoms
Re: Opening Lines

Bill, I am still working on the rest of the profiles, but I do have one for our hero, Chuck Nary. It was easy. With any luck, I'll have the rest of the character profiles done about the same time as the book. This is exciting! My mind is buzzing with great ideas for the plot.

As it turns out, Mr. Nary has a bit of a sorted past. I was thinking about giving him a scar and an eye patch due to a childhood fight with a feral cat. My friend Chet says those physical traits are more like that of a villain. Hey, how come villains in movies and books always have deformities? They always seem to be old, Russian burn victims in wheelchairs with one grotesque, milky eyeball.

Thanks,
Grady

- - - - - - - - - - - - - - - - - - - -

To: Bill Williams
From: Grady Thoms
Subject: Chuck Nary's Character Profile

Bill, here's Chuck Nary's background. I think it's pretty good. It should give you a good understanding of the protagonist.

CHUCK NARY™ PROFILE

Charles Francis Bristol was born to a runaway, Maggy Bristol, in the backseat of a Greyhound bus outside Tuscaloosa on a hot July night in 1969. No one knows when he was conceived.

Maggy was far too young and wild to care for a baby and left him with her aunt in Memphis. She would retrieve the boy four years later, something Nary didn't learn until his twenties. They moved to the Florida panhandle for a couple years until a hurricane forced them to Louisiana. A couple years later they arrived in the Gulf Coast of Texas. Chuck was eleven.

Chuck had a lot of aggression toward others, especially his mother. They were poor and he blamed her. He was made to eat generic cereal like Puffed Rice, Weedies, and Cheery-Os. Chuck and his mother fought nearly every night. He grew out his hair and spent most of his time with the older boys at the old boatyard, throwing rocks at forgotten sailboats. The boys let Chuck hang around but gave him random kidney punches and karate chops to the throat to put him in his place. He grew tough.

When he was fifteen, Chuck became too big and strong for his mother to handle. He said and did what he wanted. He put up posters in his room of bikini-clad women lying on sports cars, and there was nothing she could do about it. Chuck started to carry a pocket knife which he first used to carve his initials in trees. It soon escalated to school desks and public park benches. Chuck would never finish his sophomore year of high school, despite a respectable 2.4 GPA.

Around the same time, Maggy ran off with a man to Colorado. Chuck wouldn't see her for ten years. He was forced into a foster home which lasted about a week. He spent two months in juvenile hall when he was caught stealing a service truck. Chuck would go back again for trying to light the bowling alley on fire. He went back a third time for beating up a man dressed as a colonial soldier walking home from one of those Revolutionary War reenactments. He was self-destructive.

At eighteen, with no money or future, Chuck felt he had no choice but to join the army. He got the idea while watching the film *The Dirty Dozen*. His favorite character was the black guy. This was a turning point. It was not easy, but he learned discipline and respect. He made lifelong friendships. Best of all, he found a purpose. He had a unique ability to find people. While stationed in Korea, he tracked down a North Korean spy and personally apprehended him. He was one of the few marines with the uncanny ability to spot a North Korean in a crowd of South Koreans.

After he served his time in the military, a friend introduced Chuck to Robert Nary, a retired detective who took him under his wing. Robert saw potential in Chuck and showed him everything there was to know about being a private eye. He familiarized him with firearms and taught him how to fight in water. He showed him the little things, like how to punch a man wearing glasses without cutting your hand. Robert Nary became such a father figure to Chuck that he changed his last name. Now he was also known as Mr. Nary.

With the elder Nary's support, Chuck opened a private investigative office in Houston. His first case—find his mother. A week later, he discovered her living in Colorado Springs, single again and working as a dental assistant. Chuck Nary and his mom formed a bond that was never broken again.

Throughout his career as a PI, Chuck made a lot of friends ,but made more enemies. There were many who would like to see Mr. Nary disappear for good. He lost count of the number of people deported or in jail because of him. Some landed in the hospital; a few ended up in the cemetery. Learning to live as a killer was hard, and killing in self-defense didn't make it any easier.

Women loved Chuck Nary. They easily fell for his golden hair and soft brown eyes. They liked his large frame, six-figure income, and refined taste in whiskey and steak. Nary liked the women as well, but he was restless. His profession forced him to spend his time on the road. It was too dangerous to settle down and start a family. He never let any lady get too close. Chuck Nary would love them and leave them. They all hated him for it, but welcomed him every time he strolled back through town.

Things were starting to slow down for Chuck. He hadn't been on a case for a while. Maybe it was time to find that special gal and settle down. He was having this thought when the phone rang about the missing couple in Bolivia.

Note: Chuck Nary™—All Rights Reserved. The name Chuck Nary is trademarked. Patent pending, as soon as paperwork is submitted and pro bono attorney(s) are found.

Thanks,

Grady

- - - - - - - - - - - - - - - - - - -

To: Grady Thoms
From: Bill Williams
Re: Chuck Nary's Character Profile

Grady, I'm not sure you received my last e-mail as I told you I don't have the time to work with you on this book. You are persistent and the Chuck Nary character is unique, I will give you credit for that.

One thing I will say about your character profile is that you need to go more in-depth on his personality. Most protagonists in great fiction have flaws and shortcomings with which people can identify. Describe Chuck Nary's weaknesses.

Remember, the characters drive the story. Once they are created, let them move freely within their own world. Let them make their own choices. If they do something that is out of character, you will lose the reader. I hope this helps. E-mail me again only when the book is completed.

Regards,

Bill

- - - - - - - - - - - - - - - - - - -

To: Bill Williams
From: Grady Thoms
Subject: Nary's Weaknesses

Bill, here are Nary's weaknesses: colder climates, crossword puzzles, redheads, arsenic, and remembering dates. He eats too much red meat. He has a lack of sympathy for most animals and American Indians born after 1975. He encourages others to start chewing tobacco. His large head is not proportioned to the rest of his body. He's allergic to plums and some breeds of dogs. He's not very good at whistling. As a boy, he scored below average in the school hearing tests. He still believes there is a Big foot.

That's about it. I'm glad we're getting a complete and thorough profile of the main character. I really feel as if Chuck Nary has his own thoughts and will make his own choices. He will drive the story. Should I do a list of his strengths too?

Thanks,

Grady

- - - - - - - - - - - - - - - - - - - -

To: Bill Williams
From: Grady Thoms
Subject: Nary's Strengths

Bill, I didn't hear back from you but here are a few of Chuck Nary's strengths: strong, great sense of direction, doesn't require a lot of sleep, has a nice natural scent, uncanny ability to know when he's being followed, good with knives, and handsome (despite large head). He has a money clip with every major credit card—including Diners. Has a great repertoire of one-liners. He loves children and finds it relaxing to go to playgrounds to watch them play for hours at a time.

There are more strengths I can list if you want. I have them all written down, but I know you are busy.

Thanks,

Grady

- - - - - - - - - - - - - - - - - - - -

To: Grady Thoms
From: Bill Williams
Re: Nary's Strengths

Okay, Grady, it sounds like you are beginning to have a grasp on the main character. Now write the book! I hope to hear from you in six months or so when you have a full draft of the manuscript. Good luck!

Regards,

Bill

To: Bill Williams
From: Grady Thoms
Re: Nary's Strengths

Bill, does this mean I have a deadline in six months? Do we have a contract?
I can work with that.
Thanks,
Grady

- - - - - - - - - - - - - - - - -

To: Bill Williams
From: Grady Thoms
Subject: Nude Scene

Bill, I have a question regarding your thoughts on nude scenes in books. I
have a nude scene coming up in my novel, but I'm not sure how to describe
it. How come there are not many nude scenes in moral novels? People get
naked too. It's not a sex scene, just a nude scene.

My cousin Jesse thinks it's okay as long as I don't describe too much or
put a picture of it in my book. I think I agree. All I'm saying is that a certain
character in my book is naked when she answers the phone. I don't describe
her female parts or even say if she is attractive. I just say she's naked when
she answers the phone. She will be talking to Chuck Nary (who will be
clothed) about the disappearance of the tourists. Her nakedness never comes
up in the conversation to Mr. Nary, but the readers will know she is naked
when she is talking to him.

I don't want to offend anyone, but I also want this book to be like real
life. Let me know your thoughts.
Thanks,
Grady

- - - - - - - - - - - - - - - - -

To: Bill Williams
From: Grady Thoms
Subject: Changing Nude Scene

Bill, I can tell by your silence that you don't care for nudity in fiction. While I don't completely agree, I respect your input. I have decided to clothe my female character in the phone scene. She will now be wearing panties and a T-shirt. I will not go into great detail on what kind of panties or T-shirt she is wearing, I will just simply let the reader know they are of the regular variety—the kind you get at Target, maybe. I have decided to make her attractive, though. I think this is a fair trade-off.

I have also decided to have Chuck Nary in a bathing suit in this scene. He just got done swimming in his pool when the phone rang. They have a brief conversation that is strictly about the missing couple in Bolivia. Neither person says what they are wearing. I'm sure there have been plenty of times when we have spoken to people on the phone who were in their panties or bathing suit and we did not know it. This is just life, Bill.

Thanks,

Grady

- - - - - - - - - - - - - - - - - - -

To: Grady Thoms
From: Bill Williams
Cc: Mair Pearson
Subject: Mair Pearson

Grady, I am forwarding your e-mails to my young but talented associate, Mair Pearson. She will be able to help you with questions and keep you on track with your novel. Please send future inquiries to her.

Regards,

Bill

- - - - - - - - - - - - - - - - - - -

To: Bill Williams
Cc: Mair Pearson
From: Grady Thoms
Subject: Introduction

Hi Mair, as you probably know, my name is Grady Thoms, and I am in the middle of writing a foreign thriller called *Mr. Nary*. I grew up in Wilsonville, Oregon, where I still live. I received an American Studies degree at Chemeketa Community College in Salem. Due to my friendly demeanor and ability to ignore rejection, I gravitated toward sales. In my life, I've sold mobile phone minutes, magazine subscriptions, Amway apparel, and a drug called Xylecron (diet pills not yet legal in the US). Currently, I sell camping gear wholesale. It's low-paying work but the best job I've had as I didn't have to buy anything up front or recruit ten people. I am thirty-two.

If we will be working together, I would like to know a few things about you. How old are you? What books have you written? What is it like working for Bill? Do you wear pantsuits to work, or is it casual? (Hey, where does a lady purchase a pantsuit, is there like a Women's Wearhouse?)

Also, do you have a boyfriend?

Thanks,

Grady

- - - - - - - - - - - - - - - - - -

To: Grady Thoms
Cc: Bill Williams
From: Mair Pearson
Subject: Introduction

Mr. Thoms, it is nice to meet you. I am not an author, but I do enjoy great fiction. Recently, I read The Immortal Life of Henrietta Lacks by Rebecca Skloot. I also just reread Parade's End by Ford Madox Ford, a fantastic read.

I have been with BWA for six months (the attire is casual). Mostly, I work with our existing authors and their agents, editing and proofreading manuscripts. At times I will help to look for new talent. You are the first author I have worked with during the "creative" process. Congratulations on choosing to write a novel. I have learned it is a commitment you must renew every day.

My boss has given me strict orders not to spend much time responding to you, just a few pointers along the way. Please contact me only when absolutely necessary, as I am also busy. Bill wanted to remind you that we do not accept unsolicited manuscripts. We are using your book and inquiries as a learning tool for me, so I am happy to help now and then.

Yes, I have a boyfriend.

Mair

- - - - - - - - - - - - - - - - - - -

To: Bill Williams
Cc: Mair Pearson
From: Grady Thoms
Subject: Establishing Rules

Bill, I think it would be important to establish rules to help all of us at this point. I know you are busy, so I think these easy-to-follow guidelines will limit the amount of work on your end while allowing maximum potential and peace of mind for me.

Rules going forward:

1) I will e-mail Mair but keep Bill in the loop on each development. No offense to Mair, but she has yet to write any fiction, let alone a great work of art such as *The Missionary.*
2) BWA associates will not use fancy terminology such as "unsolicited manuscript," which no one understands.
3) Bill has final say on everything.
4) Have fun!

Thanks,
Grady

- - - - - - - - - - - - - - - - - - -

To: Bill Williams
Cc: Mair Pearson
From: Grady Thoms
Subject: Pacing

Bill, I am well into chapter 2 of my book, *Mr. Nary.* I reread the first chapter, and I'm afraid it is a bit slow. The first few chapters of your book were so well-paced and exciting. I think I may have dwelled a little too long on what Chuck Nary was eating for lunch. One of the reasons I loved *The Missionary* was your subtle inclusions of food, which I found refreshing and authentic. I tried to duplicate your culinary style, but it seems now like I'm just filling space. Take this paragraph for example:

> *Chuck Nary wanted a burger badly, one with the works. He loved lettuce, tomato, mustard, cheese, ketchup, onions, and jalapenos. But he hated pickles. This went back to his childhood. It was no one's damn business why he didn't like pickles, he just didn't. His friends who considered themselves in his inner circle asked but faced a chilly silence. Lovers wanting to know the real Chuck Nary pried to no avail. Like so many times before, the unanswered question hung in the cold mountain morning air as Nary positioned his cowboy hat to hide his eyes and moseyed out the door, never to return.*

I believe this paragraph is good in showing that Nary is a handsome rogue detective with a disdain for pickles. Yet something is not quite right with the flow. I'll keep working on it.

Also, if you think Chuck Nary is an African-American, you are wrong. Thanks,
Grady

- - - - - - - - - - - - - - - - - - -

To: Grady Thoms
From: Mair Pearson
Re: Pacing

Mr. Thoms, I am not sure what gave you the impression that we thought Chuck Nary might be an African-American, but you are right...you need to draw in the reader with interesting character development, and I doubt a paragraph about eating a cheeseburger would be useful in the book. It is important to develop characters who are compelling, because they will define your work.

Many successful authors would argue against rereading your chapters before completing the first draft. You can always make changes in the second and third drafts. If you are looking for continued assessments for your book, I think it would be in your best interest to join a writer's group in your area. You will receive honest feedback and constructive criticism.

Please only e-mail me your inquiries. Bill will not be responding.

Mair

- - - - - - - - - - - - - - - - - -

To: Bill Williams
Cc: Mair Pearson
From: Grady Thoms
Re: Pacing

Mair, the rules we all agreed upon clearly state that Bill will be kept in the loop and have final say. You can print them out and keep them nearby if you forget again.

Thanks,
Grady

- - - - - - - - - - - - - - - - - -

To: Bill Williams
Cc: Mair Pearson
From: Grady Thoms
Subject: Research

Bill, as I write my book and fill in the details with general information, I realize there are topics I don't know a lot about. For instance, a character in my book says, "Let's get down to brass tax." I'm not sure what this means exactly, but I've heard people use the expression. Brass tax must be what you get down to when you're done with federal and state taxes. It must be for a higher income bracket.

In chapter 2, I also describe a scene where Chuck Nary's attorney is trying to obtain a warrant from a judge. The attorney presents his case, but the judge says he has no grounds to issue this warrant—*after a few minutes of fruitless pleading, the attorney's eyes suddenly light up. "Your honor, I'd like to remind you of Arizona vs. Winestein." The judge massages his beard, plodding in thought. "Yes, Arizona vs. Winestein," he muses. "How could I forget? You may have your warrant."*

As far as I know, there is no actual case of Arizona vs. Winestein, I made this up. I don't know the process of obtaining a warrant, but this seems plausible, doesn't it? You always hear these types of cases brought up in court. It's always a state verses a color, like Texas vs. Brown. Who do you talk with to get information regarding the law? Who should I talk to if I need to know about general medicine or airline security or how long it takes to bake a potato? Some things I can find by searching the Internet, but a lot of these sources are unreliable.

Thanks,

Grady

- - - - - - - - - - - - - - - - - - - -

To: Grady Thoms
From: Mair Pearson
Re: Research

Mr. Thoms, I do get the sense there are a handful of subjects where you are not in the know. First off, the saying is "Let's get down to brass tacks," and it has nothing to do with the IRS.

Regarding the law, I suggest you talk with an attorney. If it is a medical scene, talk with hospital staff to gain insight. If you a writing about a private investigator, try to set up an interview with a detective. In other words, get the information you need firsthand from an expert. Most of them, I am told, are happy to help.

Another good rule for beginning authors is to stick with writing about what you know, even if that means writing a short story.

Mair

To: Mair Pearson
From: Grady Thoms
Re: Research

Mair, I do have access to experts in many various fields. If I ever need to write about amphibians or child-rearing techniques, I can talk with my cousin Jesse. If I need information on fireworks or legal coffin requirements, I can talk with my friend Chet. Unfortunately, it's the broad, college-major type topics where I find trouble.
Thanks,
Grady

- - - - - - - - - - - - - - - - - - - -

To: Bill Williams
Cc: Mair Pearson
From: Grady Thoms
Subject: Chapter Length

Hey Bill, how do you decide how long a chapter should be? I think I may be coming to a good point where I could end chapter 2. Chuck Nary just got on the plane for La Paz, with a layover in Mexico City. Should I end with the layover or begin chapter 3 with the layover? Should I even include the layover? I think I should. People would have a hard time believing there are direct flights from Houston to La Paz. The layover part isn't long. Nary orders tapas from a bar and has a nice conversation with a Spanish architect who builds bridges. It would be nice if I could start chapter 3 with him already in Bolivia.

I noticed in your book that the chapters varied nicely in length and ended at appropriate times. I wonder if you could share your secret with me. Like most people, I enjoy books with a lot of chapters, maybe twenty-five or thirty. There is nothing worse than to be halfway through a book but only on chapter 3. There was only one chapter in *The Missionary* that I thought went on too long, chapter 17, I think.

Why is it that in some books (including yours), the author uses * * * or

large spaces between scenes? Why not just start a new chapter if you're going to do this?
Thanks,
Grady

- - - - - - - - - - - - - - - - - -

To: Grady Thoms
From: Mair Pearson
Re: Chapter Length

Mr. Thoms, it has to do with style. There are many possible formats, usually decided by the publisher. When you see three asterisks, or a gap between paragraphs, it means there has been a change of POV (point of view) between characters. You cannot read the thoughts of Character A and then read the thoughts of Character B without a break. It will confuse the reader.

To be a good writer, you need to read good writing. Notice how the novelist uses point of view and try to incorporate it in your own work. Try not to worry about how long the chapters are or when they should end right now. Concentrate on learning how to write good fiction.
Mair

- - - - - - - - - - - - - - - - - -

To: Bill Williams
Cc: Mair Pearson
From: Grady Thoms
Subject: Next Step

Bill, I have completed my third chapter and I have to say, it's the best one so far. I printed the chapters and brought them along on my sales calls. No one actually had time to read it but everyone was very excited. Needless to say, it's creating a little buzz in the Willamette Valley. I included a writing sample from this chapter to give you a taste (see below). I'm still on the lookout for a writer's group to receive feedback from other writers. For now, you will have to assess my work.

This brings me to the next item of discussion. It's sort of the gorilla in the room so I will just come out and say it—let's get a contract in place. I know we have not talked formally about a deal or anything (except for the deadline you gave me), but we should probably lock something down while *Mr. Nary* picks up steam. I will leave the details and formalities up to you. Just fax it over when you have something together so you can have exclusive rights to *Mr. Nary*™ and I can start telling people when they can expect to see it in stores. Also, I'm running out of funds and could use a cash advance. A couple grand should hold me over for a few weeks.

CHAPTER 3

As the plane descended out of the clouds, passengers began to see the majestic skyline of La Paz nestled in the bosom of the Andes. It was early but Chuck Nary had not slept a wink. He perused through Sky Mall a couple times but for once, none of the inventive items looked necessary. Maybe later he would purchase the record-playing popcorn machine or get another gnome for his garden, but that would have to wait. Somewhere out there were Art and Peggy Cooper, the missing tourists from the cruise ship.

Nary's first order of business was to meet Senor Pubano, his old trusted amigo, at Hotel Rosario in the Illampu District. Pubano would be his guide and translator as they searched for clues. Nary was afraid he didn't have much time. Statistics have shown that most missing tourists from cruises either end up dead or in the hospital from food poisoning. A few might be found at the previous port where they forgot to reboard. But Nary had it on good authority that the Coopers had been kidnapped. It had been three days since they went missing. Time was of the essence.

Chuck Nary did not have trouble blending in with various cultures. He was a private eye, and it was part of his modus operandi to go unnoticed. Before coming to Bolivia, he used a tanning bed to darken his skin. He learned key words and phrases in Spanish, like "I demand information," "Where are the missing tourists?", and "Answer my question back to me in English." For clothes, he packed a traditional montera hat, a handwoven alpaca shawl, bullfighter pants, and as always, his trusty alligator boots his uncle Sal gave him. He was ready.

During the taxi ride to the hotel, Nary studied the photo of the missing tourists. He brushed over Peggy's face with his thumb. Who would want to take them? The case was puzzling to say the least. There was no ransom made. No trace of any kind. One minute, the Coopers were enjoying the sites of Bolivia from their cruise ship. The next minute, they were gone. Something did not sit right with Chuck Nary.

After forty minutes of winding along highways and potholed roads, the taxi pulled up a steep street to the Hotel Rosario. It was still early. Nary was not to meet with Pubano until eleven, so he decided to check into his room and change. His accommodations were basic and small but clean. He would have time for a shower and a warm meal.

Nary took his time in the shower. He forgot to bring soap but he did have shampoo, which was probably not as good as soap for washing the body but he would test it out. He would be trying a lot of new things on this trip. The hotel did provide towels, but they were not as big or fluffy as American towels. They were smaller. Nary would have to use two of them to dry his large frame. Now there was only one towel left. He would say something to the clerk.

Eleven o'clock was quickly approaching, so Nary put on his bullfighter pants and the alpaca shawl. He looked in the mirror and placed the montera hat on top of his head. Not bad, he thought. The shawl was heavy but provided a sense of security. He found himself speaking aloud, "Donde estan los turistas perdidos?"

Pretty good, huh Bill?

Thanks,

Grady

- - - - - - - - - - - - - - - - - - -

To: Grady Thoms
From: Mair Pearson
Re: Next Step

Mr. Thoms, I am sorry, but there will be no contract. Finish the book and then get yourself an agent. We do not deal with individual authors. The fact that we maintain communication is highly irregular. Bill has me helping you to build my experience with new authors.

I do like your attention to detail (such as the shower soap and towels). This excerpt is funny, is that what you are intending? A shawl maybe, but bullfighter pants seem silly. Have you done research on South American attire?

Mair

- - - - - - - - - - - - - - - - - - -

To: Mair Pearson
Cc: Bill Williams
From: Grady Thoms
Re: Next Step

Mair, bullfighter pants may seem funny to us in America with no culture, but it is a way of life for many others. There are many countries with different ways of dressing, speaking, disciplining children, and varying rules regarding cologne etiquette. I suppose riding a camel is "funny" to someone who has never ridden a camel. Well, my uncle has ridden a camel, and he was not laughing because it wasn't funny. It was a way for him to get to the Great Pyramids.

It will be your fault if another publishing company signs me to a lucrative deal. You will have to answer to Bill, not me.

Thanks,

Grady

- - - - - - - - - - - - - - - - - - -

To: Bill Williams
Cc: Mair Pearson
From: Grady Thoms
Subject: Agent

Bill, how do I go about selecting an agent and a publisher? Obviously, you guys have first choice to sign me just like in the NBA (National Basketball

Association). If we can't reach a deal, I'm afraid I will have to shop Mr. Nary around. I'm looking for a long-term commitment to the Chuck Nary franchise.

What do I need to have ready to pitch my book?

Thanks,

Grady

- - - - - - - - - - - - - - - - - - -

To: Grady Thoms
From: Mair Pearson
Re: Agent

Mr. Thoms, we completely support your desire to seek out other publishers, and we welcome you to do so.

Once the book is completed, here is some basic information to put into the query regarding your manuscript. Do not forget to visit the agent's website and follow the guidelines for submission. Some agents only accept snail mail, while others welcome e-mail queries. I would start with the agents who accept e-mails (it is cheaper) and move on from there.

Most will want the following information:

1) A synopsis of the book in one paragraph.
2) A description of your audience/market.
3) Other books you see as similar.

Most agents will also ask to see your bio. Since you have no experience or credentials whatsoever, I urge you not to mention anything about yourself. If you are lucky, you will be contacted by an agent. They may ask for chapter samples or the entire manuscript. If you do not wait until the book is completed to seek an agent, you may be asked for a detailed outline.

Mair

- - - - - - - - - - - - - - - - - - -

To: Mair Pearson
Cc: Bill Williams

From: Grady Thoms
Subject: Information for Prospective Agent

Mair, I have completed the profile and will begin the agent selecting process soon. What should I do if I have a dozen highly qualified candidates and they start a bidding war over my book? I suppose I go with my gut. I am not creating an outline for Mr. Nary because I plan to let the characters take control of the story. If I write an outline it means I will be controlling the story, not the characters. This goes against what Bill said.

1) SYNOPSIS: Mr. Nary, a cunning bounty hunter, travels to Bolivia to find missing tourists from a cruise ship. With dangers lurking and the borders of a landlocked country closing in, Nary must face his past while confronting the future all in the present time.

2) AUDIENCE: My book, *Mr. Nary*, is for English-speaking men and women from age sixteen to about seventy-six. This book is not for Third-World, non-English-speaking, or uneducated people, due to the complexity of technology and weaponry described.

3) OTHER SIMILAR BOOKS/AUTHORS: *The Missionary*, of course. Anything by Ian Fleming. The prose and flow is similar to John Grisham's earlier stuff. If they ever made Harrison Ford's movie *Clear and Present Danger* into a book, it would also be similar.

Besides looking for an agent, I am still on the search for a writer's group. There is not much in my area. I am anxious to read my material in front of other aspiring artists. I will let you know how the search goes.
Thanks,
Grady

- - - - - - - - - - - - - - - - - - - -

To: Grady Thoms
From: Mair Pearson
Re: Information for Prospective Agents

Mr. Thoms, be persistent in your search for the right agent and ultimately the right publisher. Remember, many successful authors were rejected several times before being published. Unfortunately, an agent will not consider you as a client until you have finished a tightly written manuscript. This includes a number of rewrites.

I am sure Bill told you to create an outline and have the profiles done before you began writing. The characters can still move truthfully within this frame. We will not force you to write an outline. Some authors prefer to let the story unfold without one. Frankly, I am curious to see how this will turn out.

The office will be closed the next few days, so have a Merry Christmas and a Happy New Year!

Mair

January

To: Bill Williams
Cc: Mair Pearson
From: Grady Thoms
Subject: Bolivian Navy

Bill, I was doing some research, and I found out there is actually a Bolivian navy. Can you believe a landlocked country has a navy? That's like if Mexico had an ice hockey team or if Cuba had a Fourth of July safety committee (I'm on the one in Wilsonville).

There are about five thousand members in the Bolivian navy. What do you suppose they do all day? At one time, Bolivia had about three hundred kilometers of land on the Pacific coast but lost it to Chile in the *War of the Pacific* in 1884. Many Bolivians are hoping to retrieve the land someday. Every March, Bolivians celebrate *Dia Del Mar* (Day of the Sea), which is basically a parade asking Chile for its coastal territories back. The Chilean government must be unimpressed because they still own the land. I cannot say that I blame them. It would have to be a really good parade to make you think about handing over a bunch of land. Also, Bolivians might want to consider having the parade in Chile—you know—where the Chileans might actually see it.

To this day, some of the people of Bolivia are bitter toward Chileans. They blame much of their social and economic problems due to being a landlocked country. That seems pretty shallow. I don't blame my parents for my having scoliosis.

Do you think I should include the *Dia Del Mar* parade in the book? Do you think Bolivian parades are similar to American parades? I wonder if they have floats or throw candy. I wonder if their politicians and real-estate agents participate by tossing cheap Frisbees while sidestepping manure left by the horses.

Thanks,

Grady

- - - - - - - - - - - - - - - - - - - -

To: Grady Thoms
From: Mair Pearson
Re: Bolivian Navy

Mr. Thoms, any time you can include authentic (but relative) cultural events in your book, your novel will become more realistic. You must do your research. I don't think you need to go into great detail about the parade. Do not make up elements you think could be true. While these tidbits are interesting, be careful about going down rabbit holes that are not relevant to the main story.

Bill and I are curious as to when Chuck Nary will realize Bolivia is a landlocked country.

Mair

- - - - - - - - - - - - - - - - - - - -

To: Mair Pearson
Cc: Bill Williams
From: Grady Thoms
Re: Bolivian Navy

Mair, Mr. Nary will not know he is in a landlocked country for a few more chapters. This is a major detail I'm using to let the tension build. The readers will know, but Chuck Nary will not. It's like what Alfred Hitchcock said about suspense vs surprise. If people are seated at a table and a bomb explodes, that is surprise. If they are seated at the table with a ticking bomb that could explode at any moment but they continue to play cards, that is suspense. The landlocked country of Bolivia is that ticking bomb.

Thanks,
Grady

- - - - - - - - - - - - - - - - - - - -

To: Bill Williams
Cc: Mair Pearson
From: Grady Thoms

Subject: Pubano Character Profile

Nary's trusted friend, Pubano, is starting to have a prominent role in the novel. I thought I'd better give him a backstory.

Pubano Profile

Pubano Domingo was born to a poor banana farmer in the late '50s near Cobija, a village in northern Bolivia. Many banana farmers can earn a decent living in Bolivia, but not the Domingos. Pubano's father, Adelmo, who wasn't very good at it. His bananas were small and never formed the natural, curvy shape. They were short and stubby. No one cares to eat small, stubby bananas. At the open markets in town, the Domingos consistently came in third in sales behind the other banana families, the Fernandos and Ricardos. Many believed Adelmo was cursed, but the real culprit was poor soil and the habit of not really caring.

Pubano was the second child of seven. He was smart but shy. While his schoolmates played cacho dice, Pubano preferred to sit at his desk and study world maps or draw submarines. He was not popular with the other students. They made fun of his small size. He did not properly develop due to a diet consisting of soybeans, stubby bananas, and three to five cups of coffee a day.

Pubano did not care to follow in his father's footsteps as a lousy banana farmer. At the age of sixteen, he packed all his belongings in a suitcase and boarded a bus for the capital. He planned to join the small but proud Bolivian navy. For the first two years, Pubano was assigned to the Rio Beni, a tributary to the Amazon River. He was part of a patrol group to help protect and guide the coca boats into Brazil. Back then, cocaine was legal and used as a stimulant for lazy plow oxen. Years later, Pubano was stationed at Lake Titicaca, where he and his shipmates spoke unknowingly about tides and currents.

When his service was done, Pubano moved to La Paz to find work. He met the beautiful but bossy daughter of a senior naval commander and quickly married her before anyone else could. He and his new wife, Alegria, opened a bakery called La Banana Chica (The Stubby Banana) to moderate success. Every evening, Pubano would carefully place a few loaves of bread in his satchel and hike up the street to the impoverished local orphanage. The delighted boys and girls ran to greet him. There, he handed the leftovers to the children while he told them facts about piranhas—like how they could strip a cow to the bone in a few minutes and how, statistically speaking, one of the children would be eaten by a pack of piranhas at some point in their lifetime.

In 2003, Pubano and his wife made the trip to San Diego when Alegria's sister went missing. A US naval captain, a friend of Alegria's father, promised them the best bounty hunter in the business. They met a hotshot private eye out of Houston who introduced himself as Mr. Nary. It took Chuck Nary only thirty-six hours to find the girl. She had run away with an older man to Las Vegas. The girl was strung out, broke, and suffered from Stuckhome Syndrome, but she was alive. Pubano pledged a life indebted to Chuck Nary and struck up a close friendship. He even flew to Texas to help Nary with a case involving members of a Bolivian crime family who intended to take out a defected high-profile soccer player. Mr. Nary and Pubano made the perfect partnership. They were able to protect the athlete while turning the thugs over to the FBI. Unfortunately, part of the job requirement was watching a lot of MLS soccer games ending in 0-0 ties.

A couple years passed before Pubano's and Nary's paths crossed. This time, Nary would be on Pubano's turf. The case would not be easy. In fact, people would die, lives would change, and country borders hung in the balance.

Pubano Weaknesses: Small frame, sometimes slow to think and act, not very good at shaving, addicted to caffeine, inability to have children, and has severe chapped lips. He associates with known futbol hooligans. He has contributed to Bolivia's deforestation. One time he framed a Chilean tourist with false animal abuse charges.

Pubano Strengths: Great with explosives, excellent swimmer, beautiful wife, impressive cigar collection, and is an efficient driver of all-terrain vehicles. He has a thirst for general knowledge. He has rich, full eyebrows. Can handle his pistol and his booze at the same time. At weddings, he is the first to tell the bride she is glowing, whether she is or not. Above all, he is loyal to Nary.

Thanks,
Grady

- - - - - - - - - - - - - - - - - - - -

To: Grady Thoms
From: Mair Pearson
Re: Pubano Character Profile

Mr. Thoms, I am glad you are creating profiles for your major characters. The writing will flow better, and the story should take care of itself within the structure you set. Frankly, I have never read profiles like the ones you create. To each his own, I guess. I will say that if your characters are having more fun than you, you are doing something right.

I do have one quick observation regarding the Pubano profile. Not that it will come up in the book, but you mentioned the missing girl had "Stuckhome Syndrome." I believe you mean "Stockholm Syndrome," referring to the phenomenon when hostages sympathize with their captors. It is an honest mistake.
Mair

- - - - - - - - - - - - - - - - - - - -

To: Mair Pearson
Cc: Bill Williams
From: Grady Thoms
Re: Pubano Character Profile

Mair, I do mean "Stuckhome Syndrome." It happens to older teenagers and young wives who live in snowy, mountainous communities. After years of staying indoors due to strict rules or the elements, they run away and go overboard, spending money in excess, eating whatever they want, and living it up. These women are hard to find because they are always on the move.

My cousin Jesse has a friend in Alaska who woke up one morning to find his wife gone. They found her six months later, wandering around a mall near Phoenix. She maxed out six credit cards. Her hair was starting to fall out from constant perms. Her hands and feet were raw from daily manicures and pedicures. She had a crazed look on her face. It was Stuckhome Syndrome. You probably won't find it on the Internet.

Thanks,

Grady

- - - - - - - - - - - - - - - - - - - -

To: Bill Williams
Cc: Mair Pearson
From. Grady Thoms
Subject: My Homage to Bill

Bill, there is a paragraph in *The Missionary* I really enjoyed. It's actually a passage that would work well in the beginning of chapter 4 of *Mr. Nary.* I may use it with a few minor changes. It would be my homage to you.

Is it common for authors who respect each other to cover each other's material like musicians? It could be like when Bob Marley covered Eric Clapton's song "I Shot the Sheriff." I want to recognize your outstanding work by incorporating it into my book. Maybe on your next novel, you could cover some of my stuff.

This is the paragraph from *The Missionary* I would like to use. It's from chapter 1:

Swarms of Latinos hurried by in the warm, humid night, seemingly unaware. Salsa music blared from one of the bars down the street. Honking cars, trucks, and buses jammed Avenue Casanova. The stink of urine rose from the gutter, a bitter note blending with the fragrance of fresh arapas, frying chiles, refried beans, and beer. "Vamonas, arribe!" someone yelled from down the street.

Here is how it will look in *Mr. Nary*. The changes are to fit the more gritty tone I have set:

Swarms of Bolivians hurried by in the warm, humid darkness, totally unaware. Violent rap music blared from one of the bars down the street. Honking jeeps, tanks, and men on llamas carrying drugs and guns jammed Avenue La Paz. The stink of urine, puke, and death rose from the gutter, a bitter note blending with the fragrance of fresh arapas, beer, and Tigress, the choice perfume of the local working girls. "Vamonas, arribe!" someone screamed from down the street while shooting a pistola into the air. (1)

The number is to cite your book. At the bottom it will say: "(1) *This paragraph is basically from The Missionary by Bill Williams.*"
Thanks,
Grady

- - - - - - - - - - - - - - - - - - - -

To: Grady Thoms
Cc: Mair Pearson
From: Bill Williams
Re: My Homage to Bill

Grady, in the music world it may be a sign of admiration to cover another artist, but in the publishing world, it is called plagiarism. You may have good intentions, but I deny you permission and insist you not put any footnote or reference to me in your manuscript.
Regards,
Bill

- - - - - - - - - - - - - - - - - - - -

To: Bill Williams
Cc: Mair Pearson
From: Grady Thoms
Subject: Upside-Down Exclamation Point

Bill, so you feel I shouldn't use your paragraph because it's not in line with "industry standards." I get it. Sometimes we have to follow the rules.

Hey, how did you create upside-down exclamation points in your book—you know, at the beginning of a sentence to show that a Latin person is yelling? My keyboard just has regular ones. I tried double-shifting, using various F numbers, and even holding the keyboard upside down while typing. The exclamation point still comes out verted; I need it *in*verted.

Thanks,

Grady

- - - - - - - - - - - - - - - - - - - -

To: Grady Thoms
From: Mair Pearson
Re: Upside-Down Exclamation Point

Grady, for Microsoft Word users, hold down the Ctrl, Alt, and Shift keys while typing the exclamation mark. This is the same for the question mark. A lot of this information is readily available on the Internet.
Mair

- - - - - - - - - - - - - - - - - - -

To: Bill Williams
Cc: Mair Pearson
From: Grady Thoms
Subject: About the Author

Bill, my "About the Author" is completed. I'll include this in the synopsis to give to prospective agents.

Grady Thoms currently lives in Wilsonville, Oregon. He will eventually reside in a cottage near Lake Tahoe with his wife and two or three beautiful children. He enjoys hiking, camping, feeding the neighbor's horses, getting mail, and staying active. He maintains a 145 bowling average.

Grady loves to travel. He has been to Portland, Seattle, San Francisco, Redding, Sacramento, and everywhere in between. Someday you might see him walking the streets of Istanbul or on a ferry in the English Chanel.

Grady has a big heart and is active in his community. He once anonymously donated two hundred dollars to Surrogate Fatherz, a nonprofit that takes inner-city children camping and brings rural children to the inner city. Every summer, he volunteers his time to lifeguard at the community pool. During his watch, zero lives have been lost.

Despite his successes, Grady Thoms is down-to-earth and approachable. He will talk to any of his fans for any amount of time. For a small fee, he is happy to sign copies of his book. He only asks that you not give your copy away when you are done reading it, and instead, he would like you to encourage others to buy their own copy.

Mr. Nary is Grady's first novel of many to come. Be on the lookout for these titles: Mr. Nary's Deadly Vacation, Mr. Nary's Dangerous Game, Mr. Nary's Even More Dangerous Game, and Alone and Scared: The Guide for Women Lost in the Woods.
Enjoy the journey,
Grady Thoms

Bill, if you need me to expand on this, I can. I took out the part about me taking third in the hurdles at a regional high school track meet. I also left out the part about our family hosting a Filipino exchange student, Huong, who accidentally killed our family cat and was sent home early.
Thanks,
Grady

To: Grady Thoms
From: Mair Pearson
Re: About the Author

Grady, you can write the "About the Author" when the book is completed. It is not very important in the scope of things, and you will only need one or two sentences. How about, *"Mr. Nary* is Grady Thoms's first novel. He currently resides in Wilsonville, OR."

It is not very flashy, but at least you will sound humble. Leave your fans wanting more. Shroud yourself in mystique.

Mair

- - - - - - - - - - - - - - - - - - - -

To: Bill Williams
Cc: Mair Pearson
From: Grady Thoms
Subject: Gypsies

Bill, what do you know about Gypsies? I want some in my book. They are just the sort of cryptic characters that would lend weight to *Mr. Nary.* As you know, some of the best songs are about Gypsy women. Gypsies are the literary equivalent to cinnamon. They make everything better. I know they live mostly in Eastern Europe, but I doubt anyone will complain if I add a few to Bolivia. Like cats, they live pretty much everywhere by now. You never know what a band of Gypsies are up to, it could be anything from bootlegging fermented goat milk to performing curses on small business owners in strip malls.

Do you know any Gypsies personally? I sure would like to interview one. If Gypsies were traveling up to Canada to sell stolen watches and invited me along, I would go. I hear they are fairly secretive. It's probably best to enjoy the Gypsy culture from a distance. I wonder if they get mad when people utter bigoted statements such as "Man, I got gypped on that ham sandwich" or "Larry, you've been acting awfully gyppy lately."

Do you think Bloodlet, Madina, and Gypsy Gary are good Gypsy names?
Thanks,
Grady

To: Grady Thoms
From: Mair Pearson
Re: Gypsies

Grady, Bill knows a lot about Gypsies. He has eight of them living in his back-yard. At night, they sing songs about living on trains and making pants out of bandanas.

Kidding aside, you need to do your own research here. I can help you with structure but not content. That needs to come from you.

Bill and I encourage you to write freely in the first draft, but later it will be essential to edit your own words so the story does not get bogged down in clutter and detail. As you reread and rewrite the manuscript, you will have to learn to strip away unnecessary descriptions, even if they are highly enter-taining (which they are).

By the way, your view of Gypsies is askew. If you want to learn about the Gypsy culture from Gypsies, a good place to start is the Gypsy Council and Roma Traveller. Ask for Gypsy Gary.
Mair

To: Bill Williams
Cc: Mair Pearson
From: Grady Thoms
Subject: Montage

Mair, I had a revelation on how I could cut fatty content without losing the meat of the story. In chapter 4, I inserted a montage. Some of my favorite scenes in movies are montages—like when a boxer is training for a fight or a new couple is getting to know each other through a series of fun dates. It allows plotlines to develop quickly. I figure why not have a montage in my book too? Unfortunately, the literary montage has no music.

In this scene, Chuck Nary and Pubano are working hard to find the missing tourists. Using some dialogue, I was able to set up the montage and then the reader's imagination will take over. It's pretty ingenious.

"I guess there will be no easy way to find the Coopers," said Nary, lifting his montera hat and wiping the sweat from his brow. "Not sure what we should to do next."

"Senooor, we chud yump in my car and go to da cheeets and rook for 'um. Chumone might know shumshing," replied Pubano. "We don reary have any reeds on da case jhet."

"I think you're right. It's time to do some legwork for the next few hours. It's going to be a long afternoon of asking questions and showing people pictures to which they will probably just shrug us away. At least we will have some inspirational music playing in our heads to provide us with some resolve and determination."

With that, Nary and Pubano headed towards Distrito Sur, a district in the southern part of the city where the sounds and smells of drug trafficking, mangoes, Gypsies, and loose women were heavy.

Author's Note: At this time the author would like you to put down the book and download the song "I Can't Hold Back" by Survivor. While the song is playing, close your eyes and think about Chuck Nary and Pubano roving the seedy parts of La Paz. They are asking questions and showing pictures to strangers. Feel free to use your imagination here—maybe Chuck Nary pushes a street tuff against a brick wall after he loses his temper. Maybe Pubano bribes a bartender with twenty Bolivianos to gain information. The better your imagination, the better your montage will be. If your montage wasn't that good, you only have yourself to blame. (Do not blame me or the band Survivor.) When the song is over, you may return to reading.

"Man, that was a long day," stated Nary as the golden light from the fading sun reflected off his grizzled face. "And we are back to where we started."

"Yesh, I'm reary tired," added Pubano. He plumped himself down on the sidewalk and shook his water canteen. He winced, realizing it was empty.

I am pretty excited with the way this turned out. There are not a lot of books that encourage reader participation without the author having to do all the work. And I was able to incorporate an actual song (which turned out sweet) for the literary montage. I don't mean to toot my own horn, but this is groundbreaking stuff.

It could revolutionize the way authors interact with their audience.
Thanks,
Grady

- - - - - - - - - - - - - - - - - - - -

To: Grady Thoms
From: Mair Pearson
Re: Montage

Grady, while I appreciate your attempt at brevity and find this highly amusing, I do not think it is a good idea to have people put down your book, download a song, and use their own imagination. You could describe Mr. Nary and Pubano searching for the tourists in just a few sentences while still showing their diligence.

Furthermore, the accent for Pubano is difficult to read and uneven. Some might say offensive. Not to stereotype how some ethnic groups speak, but did he switch from Hispanic to some sort of Asian accent in midsentence? Is he not Bolivian? I suggest you read your dialogue aloud. You will hear words differently, and it will allow you to make your characters more believable.
Mair

- - - - - - - - - - - - - - - - - - - -

To: Mair Pearson
Cc: Bill Williams
From: Grady Thoms
Subject: Pubano's Accent

Mair, this is not good news. Pubano is a major character and has a lot of dialogue. I want him to speak broken English in a Latin American accent. I'm not sure how to proceed. I was going to have Pubano stutter too, but my friend Chet says stuttering is not really a problem outside of the US.

From this point on, I will consider toning it down, but I'm not going to go back to change what I've written. That sounds like too much work.

Other than that, I'm keeping the montage. I like it.

Thanks,

Grady

- - - - - - - - - - - - - - - - - - -

To: Grady Thoms
From: Mair Pearson
Re: Pubano's Accent

Grady, you will have to amend what will be considered sloppy writing if you want to attract an agent. This highlights the value of a writing group. Others may hear nuances in the dialogue or plot that you do not. Do not be afraid to make changes, even though you are committed to your characters. You want your readers to like them too.

Mair

- - - - - - - - - - - - - - - - - - -

To: Bill Williams
Cc: Mair Pearson
From: Grady Thoms
Subject: Book Dedication

Bill, I'm encountering a predicament of colossal importance regarding to whom I should dedicate my book. I'm not married and have no brothers or sisters. I suppose I could dedicate *Mr. Nary* to my parents, but they are no longer together. I don't want to say "*To My Parents*" because that implies they are still married, and Trent (my mom's boyfriend/landlord) might not like that.

I do have a couple of people who are close to me. My cousin Jesse gave me a copy of *The Missionary*, which inspired me to write in the first place. My friend Chet has been a big supporter and helped me come up with ideas regarding plotlines. Of course, I could dedicate the book to you. *The Missionary* roused my creative juices to create a story using my own characters. You are the reason I'm realizing my lifelong dream I've had since six months ago.

You might think I'm spending too much time on this, but the dedication is the first thing people read after the All Rights Reserved page. Your dedication was so simple but eloquent—"*To Nancie.*" Most authors would have put "*To My Wife*," which is boring and impersonal. There are a billion wives out there but probably only a few thousand Nancies.
Thanks,
Grady

- - - - - - - - - - - - - - - - - - -

To: Grady Thoms
From: Mair Pearson
Re: Book Dedication

Grady, you still have plenty of time to decide on the dedication. Many authors do not think about it until their work is finished. Maybe the choice will be easier for you when *Mr. Nary* is closer to completion. Do not waste time here.
Mair

- - - - - - - - - - - - - - - - - - -

To: Mair Pearson
Cc: Bill Williams
From: Grady Thoms
Re: Book Dedication

Mair, if the dedication is the last thing written, why is it in the front? How many dedications have you written? Probably zero, unless you wrote one for your college paper, "Critiquing others who do things I will never do." And what did your dedication say—*To my mom for sending Rice Crispy Treats with my weekly laundry?*

Sometimes I need to hear from an expert.

Thanks,

Grady

- - - - - - - - - - - - - - - - - - - -

To: Grady Thoms
Cc: Mair Pearson
From: Bill Williams
Re: Book Dedication

Grady, please allow Mair to help you. She is bright and well-versed in creative writing. She is doing her best. If you cannot accept criticism and input from her, we will stop communication. Mair is upset by your flippancy toward her and asked me to assign another editor. I urged her to continue, as it's a learning tool for both of you (even though she claims to have learned nothing so far).

Regards,

Bill

- - - - - - - - - - - - - - - - - - - -

To: Bill Williams
Cc: Mair Pearson
From: Grady Thoms
Subject: Dedication Complete

Sorry Bill, I know you wouldn't hire someone untrustworthy. I figure she is e-mailing me what you tell her to anyway. I do appreciate you and Mair helping me. This book is going to be worth all the trouble. We will all be laughing at this over oysters, strawberries, and a bottle of white wine one day.

The good news is that I completed the dedication. I think I found a way to make everyone happy: "*To Jesse, Chet, and my parents, who are no longer together but loved equally; and especially to Bill for providing a deep blue sea of inspiration, a thousand ships of imagination, and a sun of warmth and support as our journey sailed to a land of fruitation.*"

I mean these words, Bill.

Thanks,

Grady

To: Grady Thoms
Cc: Mair Pearson
From: Bill Williams
Re: Book Dedication

I insist that whoever publishes this book not dedicate it to me.

Regards,

Bill

To: Bill Williams
Cc: Mair Pearson
From: Grady Thoms
Subject: Nary's Mustache

Bill, is it too late to introduce Chuck Nary's mustache? I'm in the middle of chapter 4 when I mention it: "*Nary gently stroked his well-groomed mustache as he listened to the woman recount events from a week ago.*"

Do you suppose this is more of a first- or second-chapter type description? I went back and attempted to insert it somewhere, but it was not an easy thing to do. I don't want to blindside my readers with this extra physical detail if they have something else in mind. People may have to change their visual image of him. That can be unsettling this late in the book. It's like when you meet a lady online and four months later you find out she has three cats and a child. Withholding some information is still a lie.

Maybe I should just leave the mustache out. I always imagined Chuck Nary as having one. I just failed to include it.

Thanks,

Grady

To: Grady Thoms
From: Mair Pearson
Subject: Nary's Mustache

Grady, not sure what to tell you here. It seems implausible that you cannot
insert this minor detail earlier. Most authors give a description when they
first introduce their character so the reader can visualize him or her. Then
again, I doubt this minor detail would shatter any reader's heroic image of
Mr. Nary, whether it's the first, fourth, or nineteenth chapter.
Mair

- - - - - - - - - - - - - - - - - - - -

To: Bill Williams
Cc: Mair Pearson
From: Grady Thoms
Subject: Implied Love Scene

Bill, late in chapter 4 there is an implied love scene between Pubano and his
wife Alegria. How far should I go before I cut back to Chuck Nary, who is walking the streets searching for Jabby, a drug runner? Obviously, I don't want to go
into great detail, but the love scene does need to be implied to show that Pubano
and Alegria have a healthy relationship. They are married so I think it's okay to
show some affection. Right now I have Pubano and Alegria gently kissing on
the *couche* (Spanish for couch) and he's rubbing her arm. Pubano takes off his
shoes and Alegria lets down her hair. Then they go into the bedroom.

I let my friend Chet read this excerpt and he thinks the love scene implies
nothing, really. He feels they could have gone in the bedroom and just fallen
asleep. There is no sure way for the reader to know they did anything beyond
kiss. He claims it happens with married couples all the time. They start kissing,
go to the bedroom, and then the wife falls asleep. Chet wants me to describe
more and says a semi-juicy love scene will only increase book sales. I just don't
feel real comfortable about it. As you know, I'm not married and no expert
on the subject. I suppose I could add: "*Pubano and Alegria walked into the
bedroom with their eyes locked on each other, neither one really tired at all, both
knowing their evening of marital exploration was just getting started.*"

What do you think? Intimate relationships are not my strong suit, so I really need help here. Just wait until the car chase chapter. I won't be asking for help then, I'll just let you enjoy.

Thanks,

Grady

- - - - - - - - - - - - - - - - - - - -

To: Grady Thoms
From: Bill Williams
Re: Implied Love Scene

Grady, simple affection should be enough. Most will see the connection. I would not add to it.

Mair

February

To: Bill Williams
Cc: Mair Pearson
From: Grady Thoms
Subject: Fight Scene

Bill, I'm coming to a point in chapter 5 where Chuck Nary has a fight with a guard outside the drug lord's illegal penguin-breeding compound. I've thought about it a lot and I'm afraid Mr. Nary is going to have to kill this one. He just can't keep knocking guys out with his elbow or knee. This would be the fifth one and readers might start to think this is unrealistic. Can you help me come up with a humane but creative way for Nary to dispatch this guard? I don't think Nary would shoot him or break his neck. As I stated in his character profile, Nary would only kill in self-defense. There must be a struggle.

I would like this to be a unique death. At first, I thought that Nary could stab him in the neck with his hotel pen while the guard has his fingers in Nary's eyes. He had no choice. I could minimize the blood so it's not too gory—"*Nary was surprised at how little blood flowed from the wound. His pen was even still usable.*"

Can a person even die from a minor neck stabbing? My friend Chet suggested Mr. Nary use a pencil, and the guard would eventually die from lead poisoning. I heard it takes like three or four days to die from lead poisoning (if at all), and then what would I write? "*The guard lay there bested, holding his neck with the lead already seeping into his bloodstream. He knew he had just a couple of days to say good-bye to his family and tie some loose ends up at work.*" I think we all can agree this is out. The guard should be dead when Nary leaves.

I'll tell you what I don't want. I don't want a decapitation of any kind or an explosion. His body should be intact and there should be no bones or organs visible from the fight. The family should be able to have an open coffin service for him. Bruises, bite marks, and some swelling is okay.
Thanks,
Grady

- - - - - - - - - - - - - - - - - - -

To: Grady Thoms
From: Mair Pearson
Re: Fight Scene

Grady, ask yourself the question: "What would Nary do to defend himself?"
Pretend you are standing there watching this struggle unfold. You are just
an observer; write what you see. Let the characters control the story. A fight
scene can be brutal; don't hide it.

Again, these are the types of discussions that would be good in a group.
Have you found a writer's group yet?
Mair

- - - - - - - - - - - - - - - - - - - -

To: Bill Williams
Cc: Mair Pearson
From: Grady Thoms
Subject: The Guard's Death

Bill, you probably have some ideas for how Chuck Nary should kill this
guard, but it is already written. During the fight, Nary punches the man in
the throat so hard that it causes his windpipe to collapse. The guard had
Nary pinned on his back and was about to shove a Naga Viper chili pepper
into the hero's mouth. The Naga Viper is the hottest pepper in the world.
If it touches your mouth, it will scorch and destroy your tongue. It's like
eating mace. I personally know the feeling because I've been pepper-sprayed
twice due to a miscommunication. Chuck Nary realizes if the Naga Viper
touches his mouth, he'll probably have to get his blistered tongue amputated
and wait for a transplant.

Speaking of which, Chet claims that doctors who do tongue transplants
are usually forced to give you the first tongue that comes along. He says
people who have received tongue transplants start liking food the previous
owners did. Do you think this is true? If I had to get a transplant, it would
be my luck that the donor was Indian. I'm allergic to curry.

Chuck Nary doesn't have to worry about a tongue transplant as he
found the will to give the guard a fatal jab just before the Naga Viper pepper

reached his mouth. It is not too brutal and there was no blood, just some wild convulsions and violent gasps for air.

Thanks,

Grady

- - - - - - - - - - - - - - - - - - -

To: Bill Williams
Cc: Mair Pearson
From: Grady Thoms
Subject: Curse Words

Bill, how many curse words do you think are too many? I'm through chapter 6, and I have a total of six. I've used *bitch* twice. Once it was used by a woman to call Chuck Nary a *son-of-a-bitch,* and another time it was used by Nary himself to describe a walk up a hill. I've also used *damn* twice, *hell* once, and *anus* once. There is also an instance where Nary gets into a situation he calls "pretty retarded." I don't know if this counts or not. Maybe this is not enough curse words? Again, I want the novel to simulate real life, but personally, I don't like to use this sort of language.

By the time the book is over, there will probably be about a dozen swears. Most will be used in dialogue, not from the narrator's voice. I think there will be a couple more damns and hells, one or two asses, and maybe a bastard if I can find a spot for it.

Thanks,

Grady

- - - - - - - - - - - - - - - - - - -

To: Grady Thoms
From: Mair Pearson
Re: Curse Words

Grady, I know it can be difficult, but when writing fiction, try not to impose your morals on the action and dialogue of your characters. They are speaking, not you. This is one of the joys of writing fiction. You are able to live vicariously through your characters. The protagonist could rob a bank, commandeer a jet plane, and fly off into the sunset with the gorgeous Swedish heir of the IKEA stores. It does not matter. They can do and say what they want with no repercussions. Well, almost anything. Maybe you should rethink having the protagonist use the word "retarded" in that context. It is in poor taste. But sure, twelve curse words seems about right.

To help you with your style and voice, I included times and dates of writing workshops coming to your area. I would suggest you attend as many as possible.

Mair

- - - - - - - - - - - - - - - - - - -

To: Bill Williams
Cc: Mair Pearson
From: Grady Thoms
Subject: Writer's Group

Mair, thanks for the list of workshops, I plan to sign up for the one given by Barry Lopez. It looks like he wrote a book called *Lessons from the Wolverine*. That sounds right up my alley.

In the meantime, I have some good news and bad news regarding the writer's group. The good news is that I finally found one with meetings which do not interfere with my bowling league (our team wears shirts that say "I'm your worst NightSpare"). The bad news is that the group is strictly for exotic science fiction writers.

I called the lady in charge anyway and asked if I could join the group. She wanted to know if my book was exotic science fiction. I lied and said it was. I don't even know what exotic science fiction is. Do you? I picture it to be like mystical stories about aliens like *Avatar* or *The Thing*. The people in the club are not going to be weird or anything, right?

It looks like I will have to make a few minor changes to make my book science fiction, or the members will quickly learn *Mr. Nary* does not belong. I just hope the quality of the writing shines through. I need feedback from people who will give straight answers. The first meeting is tomorrow evening. Thanks,
Grady

To: Grady Thoms
From: Mair Pearson
Re: Writer's Group

Grady, I think the people in this writing group will be as normal as you. You should say up front that you do not write science fiction. They may let you stay.

Please let us know how the meeting goes.

Mair

- - - - - - - - - - - - - - - - - - -

To: Bill Williams
Cc: Mair Pearson
From: Grady Thoms
Subject: Writer's Group Recap

Mair, the writing group did not go very well. First off, it was not exotic science fiction, it was *erotic* science fiction. I heard the lady wrong. It will be my first and last erotic science fiction meeting. I had no idea that "erotic" really means "pornographic," and combined with science fiction, it means, well, I don't really want to go into the details as I don't know your comfort level regarding these things. Let me just say I was very embarrassed and it all seemed very, very wrong.

The meeting was held at an elderly couple's home, who do not participate but allow their daughter's group to meet in the living room. I was the first to arrive as the directions from Google Maps overestimated how long it would take to drive there. Paul and Trudy, the hosts, were polite and offered me some wine and cheese. Soon, others arrived and introductions were made. We chatted about the weather and made small talk. I told them it was me who built the snowman in front of the library. Everyone seemed nice.

The leader, Dana, asked if anyone would like to share what they have been working on. I volunteered first so I could get immediate feedback. If I was going to get kicked out, at least I wouldn't have to stick around to listen to other people talk about their books. To make it science fiction, I turned Chuck Nary into a cyborg who could hold his breath for up to three minutes. I kept everything else the same.

While I read chapter 3 (my strongest entry), I noticed a few people giggling. By the end of the chapter, it was outright laughter. It was apparent these people do not understand good fiction. One lady asked why the Chuck Nary robot would even need to breathe in the first place and said holding its breath for three minutes is not very impressive by robot standards. Another man said he enjoyed my satire of the thriller genre but noted my entry painfully lacked eroticism. Then the group spent my entire allotted ten minutes talking about robot sensuality. One man wanted to know if the Mr. Nary robot had nipples. I reminded him that he was a cyborg, not a robot, so he probably had nipples. They are pretty demented people, and I got zero help regarding my book.

After I was done, I listened to several people read extremely graphic stories (again, I do not want to go into detail) of bizarre alien eroticism, which mostly made little sense. With each reading, it became more apparent I did not belong. Pretending to take notes, I started to see how many words I could make using the letters in the word FRUITATION (I got up to thirty-six).

Not all of the excerpts were completely unredeemable. I sort of enjoyed one guy's short story about a celestial planet where all our neutered and spayed dogs went after they died. On this planet, dogs were free to procreate as they had their parts back. The animals talked about their feelings and shared their painful experiences on Earth. It was kind of touching. One lady cried.

Even though a couple people said they enjoyed my "comedic" style, I came to an agreement with Dana that the group was not for me. She wished me luck and said I was welcomed back if I ever ventured into galactic eroticism. I don't think so.

So, I'm back where I started and still on the lookout for a writer's group.
Thanks,
Grady

- - - - - - - - - - - - - - - - - - - -

To: Grady Thoms
From: Mair Pearson
Re: Writer's Group Recap

Grady, this is pretty funny. It got a lot of laughs here in the office. You must see the humor in this experience. Intentional or not, your writing is funny. It's an angle you may want to explore. It seems to come naturally for you.
Mair

- - - - - - - - - - - - - - - - - - -

To: Mair Pearson
From: Grady Thoms
Re: Writer's Group Recap

Mair, I do not write humor. Like Bill, I write dramatic fiction in the foreign thriller genre.
Thanks,
Grady

- - - - - - - - - - - - - - - - - - -

To: Bill Williams
Cc: Mair Pearson
From: Grady Thoms
Subject: Metaphors

Bill, I'm at a point in chapter 7 where I need to come up with a good metaphor. The line is, "*The black asphalt streets of La Paz were hotter than* _____." Any ideas? I have three:

> "*The black asphalt streets of La Paz were hotter than the enchilada plates they serve at Mexican restaurants.*"

> "*The black asphalt streets of La Paz were hotter than the pasta plates they serve at Italian restaurants.*"

"The black asphalt streets of La Paz were hotter than a regular dinner plate they serve at regular restaurants."

Which one do you like best? I'm leaning toward the enchilada plate because it's so true. My cousin Jesse says metaphors are vital in good storytelling. As I continue on, I don't want to be stuck looking for metaphors, so yesterday I dedicated six hours to creating a bunch of them. If a metaphor occasion arises, I can go through the roster and insert the one that fits best. Here are a few.

"His arms and shoulders itched, like when you try on a sweater at a thrift store."

"They stumbled upon some bad luck, like when two beautiful people make an ugly baby."

"He started to cough and gag the way a kid does when he eats insulation thinking it was cotton candy."

"Chuck Nary's fighting skills were as ferocious as a lioness, but not quite as ferocious as a male lion because, come on, let's be realistic here."

"Her body was round, luminescent white, and had yet to be explored by man, much like the moon in 1968."

"He was confused, like when your grandma's kisses taste like buttermilk but she's supposed to be lactose intolerant."

"Chuck Nary held her tenderly, the way a worried shepherd holds his lost lamb knowing now he has just two days to prepare for the lamb cook-off."

"He tried to fake a smile but his insincerity was transparent, like when your girlfriend surprises you with tickets to see Jewel in concert and she invites her friends Linda and Steve. But you hate Linda and Steve."

These are pretty good at making the reader feel the emotions of the characters. I won't be using all of these, of course, but it's good to know I have a whole arsenal ready for almost any metaphor-needing occurrence.
Thanks,
Grady

- - - - - - - - - - - - - - - - - - - -

To: Grady Thoms
From: Mair Pearson
Re: Metaphors

Grady, most of what you are describing here are not metaphors, but similes. Similes use the word *like*, as in "Chuck Nary fought like a grizzly bear." A metaphor states the noun as *is*: "Chuck Nary *is* a grizzly bear." Both paint a certain picture, but metaphors tend to be more powerful. Try to limit their use and keep metaphors/similes true to the characters or objects. Do not turn Chuck Nary into a lion, then an eagle, then a locomotive, and then a warm blanket.

Your similes are way over the top, like the acting in a Michael Bay film. Perfect for your novel, I suppose.
Mair

- - - - - - - - - - - - - - - - - - - -

To: Bill Williams
Cc: Mair Pearson
From: Grady Thoms
Subject: Adding Big Words

Bill, I'm going back through the first seven chapters of the manuscript and adding big words in various spots to make the characters and the narration sound smarter. I added *copious, nepotism, transgender,* and *machinery.* I also made a reference to former tennis star Martina Navratilova. Do you have any suggestions of other big words which would sound great in a foreign thriller? Please include definitions.
Thanks,
Grady

To: Grady Thoms
From: Mair Pearson
Re: Adding Big Words

Grady, George Orwell said to never use a long word when a short one will do. Small words often have a bigger impact. They add clarity. Keep it simple.
Mair

- - - - - - - - - - - - - - - - - - -

To: Mair Pearson
From: Grady Thoms
Re: Adding Big Words

Mair, I really don't care what George Orwell has to say about good writing. While I respect him for his radio contributions and that *Citizen Kane* movie, I would hardly call him an expert in proper prose exposition and so on and such.
Thanks,
Grady

- - - - - - - - - - - - - - - - - - -

To: Mair Pearson
Cc: Bill Williams
From: Grady Thoms
Subject: Writing Workshop

Mair, a workshop might be a good place to sharpen your writing skills, but it's a terrible place to meet women. I understand this is not the main objective for attending a workshop, but I figure I'll have to meet the mother of my two sons somewhere. I look for her when strolling through the mall, getting a haircut, or throwing the Frisbee around with myself at the park. Why not look for her at the writing workshop too? I quickly deduced she was not there, however, as all the females in attendance were gray and a bit weathered. One lady was even using a picnic basket to carry her writing supplies. That sort of behavior starts around fifty-five.

It was probably a blessing there were no attractive girls. Now I could focus on my book and not have to run out to the van to change into my good sweater. I always bring my lucky sweater in case I see a girl who could be a potential mate. It's a soft white sweater which bulks up my shoulders and makes my face look tan. I must throw that sweater on three or four times a week.

Thanks,

Grady

- - - - - - - - - - - - - - - - - - -

To: Grady Thoms
From: Mair Pearson
Re: Writing Workshop

Grady, you only mentioned your attempts (and poor ones, I might add) at meeting women. What did you learn at the workshop? What sort of exercises did you do? How will it affect your writing?
Mair

- - - - - - - - - - - - - - - - - - -

To: Mair Pearson
From: Grady Thoms
Subject: Writing Workshop

Mair, the writing workshop was good. Barry Lopez told us democracy was failing. Did you know this?

Thanks,

Grady

- - - - - - - - - - - - - - - - - - -

To: Bill Williams
Cc: Mair Pearson
From: Grady Thoms
Subject: Writer's Block

Bill, they say it happens to every good writer, and it finally got to me—the dreaded writer's block. Yesterday I sat at the computer for three hours trying to finish a scene where Chuck Nary interrogates a mute orphan. The creative film reel in my brain melted, and the words are no longer there. I am hanging on a cliff of desperation. This is what I have leading up to the interrogation:

Chuck Nary escorted the scrawny, yet defiant child to the nun's office. The boy, only known as Pey, was well connected with the drug dealers in the area. They used him for the important deliveries in the Centro. Pey was trustworthy. Not only was he fearless and mean, he was also mute. Chances of him ratting out the others were slim. Even though he was a mute, no one ever called Pey dumb. He could add faster than a computer and subtract almost as fast. He was not great at fractions, but fractions were low priority in the La Paz school districts.

Mr. Nary felt Pey might know something about the recent kidnappings in the region. He sat the boy down at the nun's shoddy oversized metal desk and thumped a pen down on a waiting sheet of paper.

"Write!" Nary began pacing to the other side of the room, his arms folded over his puffed chest. Pey remained motionless. Perhaps he did not understand. "Escribal!" Nary huffed. It was the incorrect word for his command, but it was close enough. When you're Chuck Nary, people have a way of understanding you.

Pey casually crumpled up a piece of paper, careful not to lose eye contact, and flung it at the blanco's giant head. By sheer instinct, Nary wheeled his body to the side and crouched in an attack position. As the wadded ball approached, he leaped up and blocked the paper with his forearm, sending it hard to the wall.

"Don't ever do that again, kid. I could have killed you," stated Nary, barely out of breath.

This is all I've got. After that, I just stare at the computer screen. I have no idea what will happen next. I feel as if Nary and Pey have stopped and are now looking at me, waiting for direction. All I think about is Pey turning into a wild gremlin to attack Nary. But this is not that kind of story. Please help.

Thanks,

Grady

To: Grady Thoms
From: Mair Pearson
Re: Writer's Block

Grady, writer's block is common, and we sympathize. While there is no sure way for a cure, there are a few ways to approach it. Think of it as having the hiccups. Some techniques may work and others may not, but you will eventually stumble onto a solution. For now, I suggest you move away from the computer when you get stuck. Go for a walk, call a friend, or try e-mailing other publishers.

To avoid slumps in the future, it's important to develop a routine. All great writers have a routine. They start at the same time each day. They might work in their favorite room or listen to a certain kind of music. Try to find the routine that works best for you, and stick with it. Eliminate distractions and force yourself to write something, anything, even if it's not very good. You can always edit later.

Again, I found your latest entry humorous. You might want to think about promoting this as a quirky comedy.

Mair

To: Mair Pearson
From: Grady Thoms
Re: Writer's Block

Mair, finding humor in intense situations is a defense mechanism. It's like when you go to a horror movie and you hear people laughing when a teenager is murdered in the dark woods but you know they're really scared, not to mention they probably feel terrible for that teenager's family. It's okay

for you to deal with your feelings about my book by calling it funny.
Thanks,
Grady

- - - - - - - - - - - - - - - - - - - -

To: Bill Williams
Cc: Mair Pearson
From: Grady Thoms
Subject: The Mute Orphan

Bill, I let my cousin Jesse read the scene with Chuck Nary and Pey, the mute orphan, to see if he could help with the writer's block. He had a few ideas but was more concerned with the content. He thinks I should be cautious about using the only mute in my story as a mean, drug-running kid. Jesse believes I may have certain advocacy groups speaking out against the book. He claims mutes have more advocates than other groups because they do not speak for themselves. Do you think this is true? Personally, I don't think they are easily offended. If they were, they would've made a fuss about television remotes having a "mute" button. They seem okay with it. The word "blind" doesn't appear on the screen when you turn down the contrast. That would be offensive. I have a feeling the mute community is pretty laid-back.

Just to be safe, I added a disclaimer at the end of the chapter: "*The author would like to take this time to express he does not feel all mutes are mean or involved with drugs. Moreover, he would like to point out that Pey is a hearing mute, not a deaf mute, and remind the hearing impaired that this is not your fight anyway. Your protests would be without merit. While the author does not personally know any mute people, he understands it's a quiet community of valuable members to our society.*" (And then I would include a drawing of a person with xxx over his mouth holding hands with a person singing to show unity.)

Jesse says I should either add a pleasant mute to offset the mean one or redeem Pey's character who eventually assists Chuck Nary in the case. I do like the idea of Pey turning into an informant. Pey, Nary, and Pubano could be quite the force for good. This is the route I am leaning toward. Hey, I

just got an idea for the interrogation scene. Thank you for helping with the writer's block!
Thanks,
Grady

- - - - - - - - - - - - - - - - - - -

To: Grady Thoms
From: Mair Pearson
Re: The Mute Orphan

Grady, if by some small chance your book gets published, sells a few copies, and one of them lands in the lap of a mute person, I do not believe that person would see any correlation with his or her impairment and Pey's decision to sell drugs. No disclaimer is necessary.
Mair

- - - - - - - - - - - - - - - - - - -

To: Bill Williams
Cc: Mair Pearson
From: Grady Thoms
Subject: Routine

Bill, you stated earlier through Mair that it's important to establish a routine. I'm trying to develop one and was wondering if you would share yours.

Here is my routine: Before I sit at the computer, I light an ocean-scented candle. I hear many authors like to work at their beach house because of the tranquility of the ocean. For music, I play Steve Winwood's *Back in the High Life,* an album which has comforted me during three breakups, five job changes, and two major surgeries. While writing, I wear sweats and a soft cotton T-shirt without sleeves. The sleeveless shirt limits armpit rashing. I tend to move my upper body a lot when I type.

Near my computer, I usually have Goldfish crackers or Red Vines handy. There are also two types of drinks available at all times—hot tea and grape soda. Grape soda reminds me of when I was a kid and my mother used to give me Robitussin to settle my hyperactivity. Those were good memories. When I'm thinking, I'll pace around the room and throw a bouncy ball against the wall. Sometimes I lose the bouncy ball and spend up to twenty minutes looking for it.

Bill, it would be great if you shared your routine with me. I think we could learn a lot from each other. We should not be in competition. Your style is different. You have a more basic tone that is easier for novice readers. My style is more complex with compelling characters involved in an intricate plot. I think *The Missionary* is a perfect stepping-stone to *Mr. Nary.* We should think about selling them together as a package to high schools. *The Missionary* would be given out to freshman and older kids on the wrestling team. *Mr. Nary* would be given to juniors and seniors once they showed a certain amount of maturity.

Thanks,

Grady

- - - - - - - - - - - - - - - - - - -

To: Grady Thoms
Cc: Mair Pearson
From: Bill Williams
Re: Routine

Grady, Mair is right, routines are important. Every morning, I will lock myself in the office and force myself to write, even when I don't feel like it. I feel it is an accomplishment to write 1000–1500 words during this time. When writing, I will have coffee but nothing else. I certainly don't have scented candles.

Regards,

Bill

- - - - - - - - - - - - - - - - - - -

To: Bill Williams
Cc: Mair Pearson
From: Grady Thoms
Subject: Pey Profile

Bill, I created a character profile for Pey. You will notice I put his muteness as both a strength and a weakness.

Pey Profile

Pey was the product of a love affair between a prominent senator of the Bolivian Plurinational Legislative Branch and a young maid of the Camino Real, a beautiful four-star hotel with a high user rating on TravelSouthAmerica.com. Lola, the maid, caught the senator's eye from across the room during a luncheon at the hotel. Senator Guyer did not care much for the veal that afternoon, but he liked what he saw in the staff. Numbers were exchanged.

For three months, Senator Guyer would leave his office at noon to visit Lola at the Camino Real. They loved on each other in many of the rooms on the sixth floor. He showered her with costume jewelry and compliments. They watched television and ordered room service. For one or two hours, he belonged to Lola. She felt loved, but it was short-lived.

Soon, Lola began to get sick in the morning. Her regular menstruation stopped. She had cravings for cheese bread and peanut butter and started to gain weight. Her breasts would periodically get swollen and tender. She felt tired and fatigued. Lola had headaches, frequent urination, and the darkening of the areolas. She was probably pregnant.

Hearing the news, Senator Guyer ended the affair. He was married, and reelections were approaching. He could not afford another setback after his cockfighting, cocaine, and bribery scandals. However, he would not completely abandon her. Abortion is illegal in Bolivia, so the senator sent her to live with a trusted friend in the southern town of Oruro. He paid for Lola's medical bills and even sent her well wishes. The senator would never seek her out, despite losing the next election in a landslide.

Lola decided not to keep the boy she birthed on that chilly August day. In her culture, it was shameful to raise a child alone. She returned to the city and drove to an orphanage she remembered seeing near La Banana Chica, her favorite bakery. The baby carrier was left on the doorstep with the child wrapped in a towel with the initials P.E.Y. No note was included.

The caretakers of La Esperanza Orphanage thought it was odd the baby never cried. Weeks turned to months and the months into years, but he never made a sound. Pey excelled in reading, writing, and arithmetic, but he refused to talk. He was a hearing mute.

Pey became bored with the mundane schoolwork and started to develop a mean streak. He rigged chairs by breaking the legs and gluing them back on hastily. When a child sat down, he or she would crumble into a splintered heap of wooden fragments and tears. Pey mocked and made wild gestures while pointing at his victim. He did it all with no sound.

A local drug runner by the name of Jabby had been watching Pey's antics in the orphanage courtyard. Jabby liked his attitude, but he liked his silence more. He needed a new recruit when his last drug runner left to pursue other interests.

Pey grew tired of tormenting the others at the orphanage. He needed a challenge. When Jabby slipped him a note through the fence asking him if he would like to join the big boys, Pey jumped at the chance. He snuck away from the orphanage each afternoon. Pey was so quiet, Madre Isabel and the other nuns never knew when he was there and when he was not.

The silent orphan did well for Jabby. He delivered the goods quietly and always on time. Even when the local police caught and interrogated him, they faced a tiny, mute stone wall. He remained fearless and defiant with no moral compass. He never had a father figure to direct him, until the day Mr. Nary pulled him into the nun's office, that is.

Pey's Weaknesses: Mute, ornery, scrawny, picky eater, beady eyes, small hands and has a disregard for orphanage property. Taunts his teachers with notes saying he's hidden a scab somewhere around their desk. Refuses to participate in the annual plant-a-tree program.

Pey's Strengths: Mute, redeemable, clever, has ingenuity, speedy runner, expressive eyes, and math genius. Shows some interest in the piano. He is a pretty snazzy dresser as far as orphans go. Although he delivers drugs, he refuses to use them. He does not give in to peer pressure. Responds well to men with facial hair who lead by example.

Thanks,
Grady

- - - - - - - - - - - - - - - - - - -

To: Grady Thoms
From: Mair Pearson
Re: Pey Profile

Grady, I have to say, I have never read any character profiles quite like yours. Just out of curiosity, did you just list every single symptom of pregnancy from a book or off of a website? That was a thorough examination.
Mair

- - - - - - - - - - - - - - - - - - -

To: Bill Williams
Cc: Mair Pearson
From: Grady Thoms
Subject: Chuck Nary Finds Out Bolivia Is a Landlocked Country

Bill, I'm at the crucial point in the novel when Chuck Nary realizes Bolivia is a landlocked country. There is no port to dock cruise ships and no kidnapped couple. It was a trap! I want the reader to be blindsided and thinking *nooooo waaaay* when this critical piece of information is revealed.

At this point in the novel, Nary wants to go to the port where the cruise ship unloaded passengers. If the ship is back at port, maybe he could talk with the staff and establish a timeline. The trip produces a heartbreaking revelation where Nary and Pubano's relationship must endure the ultimate test. Chapter 9 ends on a major cliffhanger.

Madre Isabel was kind enough to loan Chuck Nary and Pubano the orphanage van. The American was precarious, but she sensed tenderness in his soft, brown eyes. Even though he acted in ways she had never seen, like changing his shirt in front of people, she could tell he cared for the children. Madre Isabel handed him the keys. If only she could hand him the keys to her heart too, she thought. But no, her service was to the children.

Mr. Nary promised to have the vehicle back by the next afternoon for their field trip to the soybean factory. He requested for Pey to come along and swore they would not be in danger. He just wanted to make some inquiries, he assured her. Reluctantly, Isabel allowed Pey to go.

* * *

(Bill, you will notice I used the three asterisk thingy here to show a different point of view. We are now switching from Madre Isabel to Chuck Nary.)

With the van loaded with provisions, Mr. Nary climbed into the passenger seat. Pubano waited in the driver seat for instruction. "Go west," said Nary, pointing in a direction that was exactly west. Pubano shook his head in amazement with the gringo's acute orientation in a foreign land. The old passenger van pulled onto Route 3.

Out of habit, Chuck Nary was quiet about the case, revealing only a few details to his partner. He told Pubano they were looking for a missing American couple who had come by boat. After that, Pubano was on a need-to-know basis. In fact, Nary himself did not know much more. He had names, a photo, and a few hunches. Drugs might be involved, but he needed more information. It was time to visit the spot where they were last seen.

In a little over an hour, the van lugged into the lively town of Desaguadero. Nary stirred from his nap as they approached a scaffold with a banner proclaiming, "Gracias Por Su Visita." On the other side of the small waterway, uniformed guards stood next to a checkpoint. Cars, foot travelers, and locals riding pack animals handed the men papers. Nary admired the llamas in South America. Despite the horrible smell and incessant spitting, they were perfect for carrying stuff, as long as you didn't need to arrive at your destination too fast.

"Stop the car." Nary stepped out to assess the scene. Natives wrapped in blankets traversed by, their brown noses and cheeks chapped from the harsh winds. He had been careful to not mention to Pubano he found some of the people in his country unsightly.

Climbing up the van ladder, Nary peered out into the distance. He could see the deep blue colors of Lake Titicaca. Farther away, golden brown mountains, the color of perfectly roasted marshmallows, shot up toward a handful of white fluffy clouds, which looked like regular marshmallows. There was no ocean.

"Where are we?" Nary poked his head upside down in the driver-side window.

"Da border, Senor."

"Of what?"

"Perru." Pubano's voice quaked. He could see his amigo becoming impatient. Nary jumped off the van and slid back in the passenger seat. He rubbed his eyes.

"I don't want to go to Peru, Pubano. We must have gotten lost. Turn around."

"Senor, maybe you chud tell me where we go. I cud help."

"Just drive, I'll fill you in on the way. Do you have a map in here?"

"No," replied Pubano as he executed a perfect three-point turn. Pey, eager to help Nary, pulled out his tattered notebook with Michael Jackson drinking a Pepsi on the cover and began to draw a map of Bolivia as best as he could remember.

Halfway back to La Paz, Nary spotted a sign:

Carretera de Montana
La Frontera Tambo Quemado
Oceano Pacifico

"Turn here, Pubano, that's where we need to go." Chuck Nary licked his lips. They were getting close to the ocean now. He began to think about all the questions he would pose to the captain, the bartender, the events coordinator, the youth activities coordinator, and all the other patrons. If someone knew something, he would find out. He would ask to see Art and Peggy Cooper's quarters. If there was a clue, he would find it. There had to be a reason they were taken. Perhaps the Coopers had a secret past which led to their disappearance.

"Pubano, it's time we visit the port," Nary began. "When we get on that cruise ship, I want you to be on the lookout. Observe the people and their reactions as I ask questions. Things might get heated, so be ready. I'm going to get some answers."

* * *

Pubano was confused by Nary's statement but said nothing. He had questions but did not want to upset his friend any longer. He knew Nary had been working the case for a few days straight and was exhausted.

* * *

Nary noticed that Pubano looked confused. He would explain everything once they arrived at the cruise ship. Now was the time for sleep. He drifted off, drooling on his alpaca shawl.

The pass to Tambo Quemado headed south for a couple hours and then meandered west. The road was windy and slow. Pubano carefully steered the vehicle around overloaded buses and flatbed trucks. At one point, they waded through a herd of sheep. Eventually, the van reached the high plains and the road straightened out. Chuck Nary and his companions were close to some answers, but maybe not the ones they were looking for.

Mr. Nary woke to Pey leaning over his chair, shaking his shoulder. He handed him a slip of paper with a drawing of Bolivia. It was remarkably accurate. Unfortunately, it had no roads or towns for reference, just an outline of the country with what looked like a rooster sitting on a fence. When he got home, Nary would display it on his refrigerator for a couple weeks before taking it down, which is a widely acceptable time period for throwing away children's art in Texas. Nary thanked the boy and raised the incline of his chair, hoping to see the

Pacific Ocean. Instead, they approached the town of Tambo Quemado. More ominous mountains loomed in the distance.

"How much farther do we have to go?"

"I donno, Senor. I donno where we go." Pubano was red.

"The port, Pubano. I want to go to the cruise ship where the Coopers were staying. This is your country, you're my guide. Where do cruise ships dock in Bolivia? That's where I want to go."

"Whaa?" stammered Pubano.

The van crawled through the sleepy village. Another gate with more stoic men in fatigues guarded the road in front of them. Two large flags that were not Bolivian whipped in the cool breeze. White peaks, larger the ones they had just conquered, poked sharply in the sky before them. Again, there was no ocean.

"What is this?" Nary whispered. "I don't understand. What the hell is going on?"

"Senor," Pubano gulped. "We are at the border."

It was not the answer Nary wanted to hear. He gritted his teeth.

"Of what?" Nary's fists became rocks as he embraced for an answer. Pubano stopped the van and turned off the ignition. The air grew heavy.

"Senor, I..." He paused while removing his cap. "I donno wha you wan."

Nary dropped his tone an octave. "Where are we?"

"Dis es da border. Es Chile."

Nary swatted away the lie, shaking his head.

"Chile? How can that be? Where is the port where the cruise ships dock? Pubano, where is the ocean?!"

"Senor ...Bolivia...has no ocean." Pubano dropped his head in shame. A single tear rolled down his cheek. "We loss it en da War of Pacifico to Chile in 1880. We have no coas'."

"I thought you were in the Bolivian navy!"

"I was. We patrol the lakes han rivers." Pubano's sniffles turned to a quiet sob.

"No...no." Nary's inflection teetered. "Nooooooooooo!" He slapped the dashboard with his palm. Pubano continued to cry. Pey listened *intently from the backseat. He remained silent.*

The gravity of the situation began to sink in. Flinging the passenger-side door open, Nary leaped out, cursing at the sky. He'd been had. Awkwardly, he crumpled into a sitting position on the curb and rubbed his temples with his fingers. His head pounded. Behind him in the town square, old men danced while blowing their pan flutes. The music mocked Mr. Nary. He had been set up. The country, his mind, the case…all became landlocked.

* * *

From down the road, a black SUV idled. The car had been monitoring them all day. Inside, two men began to make preparations. One lit a cigar and punched a few numbers on an outdated car phone, the other loaded his high-caliber rifle.

(turn page for chapter 10)

Pretty intense, huh? My heart was pounding while I wrote it. I don't even know what's going to happen next, so I am as excited as you.

Thanks,

Grady

- - - - - - - - - - - - - - - - - - - -

To: Grady Thoms
From: Mair Pearson
Re: Chuck Nary Finds Out Bolivia Is a Landlocked Country

Grady, your style is uncommon and, at times, appealing. It almost carries a satirical tone. I enjoyed a lot of the content, but the technique needs work. I have many notes but will present just a few for you to chew on.

The narrator should avoid using the words "things" and "stuff" to describe things and stuff. It is a bit careless and vague. What is it you are seeing exactly? Tell us.

Be careful of using too many adverbs (the ones ending in "ly") such as eventually, the van reached the high plains and the white peaks poked sharply in the sky. Adverbs are often overused and redundant. Most can be axed.

We already assume the white peaks would poke "sharply" in the sky. There is no other way to poke something.

While you have an interesting premise in chapter 9 and some decent dialogue, you need to do a better job of "showing" rather than "telling." Instead of saying "The old passenger van pulled onto Route 3," you could say something to the effect of "With loose bolts, dank carpeting, and foam protruding from torn seats, the fifteen-passenger behemoth rattled onto Route 3." The first sentence is telling us the van is departing. The second sentence, while not perfect, is attempting to put the reader inside the van. Showing takes a lot of practice and hard work. You will especially need to work on this during the second, third, and fourth drafts.

Finally, you do not need to remind readers to turn the page to chapter 10. This is not a choose-your-own-adventure.

Mair

- - - - - - - - - - - - - - - - - - - -

To: Mair Pearson
From: Grady Thoms
Re: Chuck Nary Finds Out Bolivia Is a Landlocked Country

Mair, thanks for the tips regarding the adverbs. And you make a good point regarding showing and telling, but I disagree on their use. Writers need to show *and* tell. When I was in the second grade and brought my grandpa's eye patch to class to share with the other students, I showed *and* told them. If I just showed the eye patch without telling the story of him getting stabbed in the eye with a fork by a cook during a bar fight, they would be missing the whole story. That's why they call it "show and tell." It's not just called "show."

That being said, I was impressed with the line you wrote about the van. It did create a strong visual. I would like to use it if you have no objections.

Thanks,
Grady

- - - - - - - - - - - - - - - - - - - -

To: Grady Thoms
From: Mair Pearson
Re: Chuck Nary Finds Out Bolivia Is a Landlocked Country

You can use my line if you want, Grady, but I think you missed the point of showing versus telling in fiction. It has nothing to do with sharing family heirlooms with your classmates in the second grade.
Mair

- - - - - - - - - - - - - - - - - - -

To: Bill Williams
Cc: Mair Pearson
From: Grady Thoms
Subject: Map of Bolivia

Bill and Mair, do you think I should include a map of Bolivia at this point? In chapter 9, there is a lot of driving, various highways, different villages, and three countries involved. I always liked that JR Tolkien included a drawing of Middle Earth as a reference point for the readers of *The Hobbit* and LOTR. Maybe I'll do the same for MN.

I let my friend Chet read chapter 9, and he was confused by the geography. He thinks it's impossible for Chuck Nary and the others to travel to Peru and Chile from Bolivia in one afternoon. I told him it was very possible. We got into a geography argument which led to a heated game of *Risk*. After a few hours we had to quit because Chet loaded Australia with all of his armies and I could never overtake it. Chet is a cheater.

If we do use a map, do you think it should have a dotted line to show where the van has traveled? It could be like one of those Family Circus comic strips where you follow Billy around the neighborhood. I don't want anyone lost going into chapter 10, when the foreshadowings and allegories are turned up a notch.
Thanks,
Grady

- - - - - - - - - - - - - - - - - - -

To: Grady Thoms
From: Mair Pearson
Re: Map of Bolivia

Grady, using a map is up to you. Your novel is unconventional in many ways, so I do not see a problem with you including one.

The mentioning of allegories in your novel has me curious—could you list some you have or plan to use? Why do you feel it's important to use an allegory? I do enjoy the depth they add to storytelling.
Mair

- - - - - - - - - - - - - - - - - - -

To: Mair Pearson
From: Grady Thoms
Subject: Allegories

Mair, I am puzzled that you have not picked up on any of the allegories in *Mr. Nary* thus far. I figured an English major of your caliber would easily see the rich symbolism soaked within the sample chapters I have submitted. One obvious allegory is that Chuck Nary represents America during the Industrial Revolution. When it comes to investigating, Nary is "progressive," has a "machine"-like work ethic, and uses a "factory" of resources. Plus, he looks a bit like a young Andrew Carnegie.

Another allegory is that Chuck Nary represents the future because you don't really know what's going to happen next. Lastly, Chuck Nary is a symbol for the ocean because he's mysterious and dangerous. This becomes clear by Pubano's respect and admiration for him.
Thanks,
Grady

- - - - - - - - - - - - - - - - - - -

To: Grady Thoms
From: Mair Pearson
Re: Allegories

Grady, so Chuck Nary is a thinly veiled symbol for the Industrial Revolution, the future, and the ocean. Got it.

I printed out chapter 9 to make additional notations, and something unexpected happened. Without my knowledge, a coworker of mine plucked it from the printer and began to read it aloud to other staff members in the break room. Before you get upset, you should know they all found it very amusing and asked to read more. Ed Simmons, an accountant and prolific reader of thrillers, used the word "fascinating." Is it okay if allow them to read our past correspondence?
Mair

- - - - - - - - - - - - - - - - - -

To: Mair Pearson
Cc: Bill WIlliams
From: Grady Thoms
Re: Allegories

Mair, they can read whatever they want but I only care for Bill's opinion and sometimes your opinion. Has he read chapter 9 yet?
Thanks,
Grady

- - - - - - - - - - - - - - - - - -

To: Grady Thoms
Cc: Bill WIlliams
From: Mair Pearson
Re: Allegories

Grady, Bill did read your chapter and was grinning the entire time. I think we may be on to something here, but not necessarily in the exact way you may intend. We will talk more in the future. Continue to work on the book and keep us updated.
Mair

- - - - - - - - - - - - - - - - - -

To: Mair Pearson
Cc: Bill Williams
From: Grady Thoms
Subject: Woman Advice

Mair, I'm glad you think we are on to something but Bill and I have always known it's a quality project. Tell your associates at BWA they will have to wait a couple days to find out what happens in chapter 10, which is showing early signs of promise. In the meantime, I could use some council from a woman in our age demographic. Maybe you can help.

There is a pleasant-looking lady in my apartment building who I believe is single. Her name is Jenny. I know this because her cable bill accidentally landed in my mailbox last week. She must make decent money because, according to her bill, she subscribes to HBO, Showtime, and rented seven movies-on-demand last month (she watched *Love in the Time of Cholera* twice). Jenny seems really nice. We smile and say hello but have yet to really talk. She smells great, which if I am not mistaken, is Herbal Essence shampoo. If I'm right, I have an icebreaker.

When we finally strike up a conversation, I want to impress her. Is it too early to tell her I'm an author? Would it be a lie if I told her I was a successful author? Technically, my book could become a best seller and then it would be true. I don't want to tell her I'm in camping gear sales. All the women I know hate camping. My cousin Jesse says I should stop telling women I meet that I can get them discounts on sleeping bags. He thinks it sounds creepy. He also says I should start cleaning out the back of my van of all camping supplies and samples when I take a girl on a date. I have flashlights, shovels, duct tape, rope, pocket knives, and books on knot tying back there. I guess women are intimidated by men who can survive for weeks in the wilderness.

This might be an impossible favor to ask, but is there any way to get an advanced copy of my book? I'll pay whatever. I realize *Mr. Nary* is not done, but I figure we could repeat the nine chapters I do have until it's about three hundred pages. I just want the book on my shelf in case Jenny ever comes over to my apartment. It will give me something to point to and pick up

while I talk about our profession and the misconceptions people have about authors.
Thanks,
Grady

- - - - - - - - - - - - - - - - - - - -

To: Grady Thoms
From: Mair Pearson
Re: Woman Advice

Grady, I am not a relationship expert, but I do know that you should not tell this woman you are an author. You could tell her you are aspiring to be one or that writing is a hobby.

I believe you can start telling people you are an author when you publish a book and it has sold at least one copy.
Mair

March

To: Bill Williams
Cc: Mair Pearson
From: Grady Thoms
Subject: Plot Points

Bill and Mair, I'm going to clue you two in on a few secrets so you can tell me if you see any holes. Remember Sophia, the woman in the first chapter who phoned Chuck Nary while in her panties? She was the one who set him up with the bogus case. Sophia is avenging her brother's death who became a fugitive after being suspected of smuggling opium using bottles from the hairspray brand *Hair Owen*—which turned out to be an unfortunate coincidence for him.

Contracted by the government, Nary tracked the brother down and handed him over to the authorities. Within days, he was murdered by a fellow inmate with Mafia ties, as he was suspected of owing them money. Sophia blames Mr. Nary and hatches a plan for vengeance. She has connections in Bolivia. That is why she sent him there. However, it has not been easy for the hired guns. Nary's unpredictable movements and complete integration into the Bolivian culture have made him difficult to track down.

While Nary and Pubano were looking for the fictional couple, they crossed a powerful drug lord who uses street orphans to transport drugs. He was using stray dogs, but they became pretty unreliable. Nary learns of Senior Hugo Hector Raul, the most feared and dangerous of all the drug kings in La Paz. It was rumored Hector Raul would kidnap tourists to use as ransom if his drug shipments were confiscated. Following a hunch, Nary went to one of his drug compounds to look for Art and Peggy Cooper. He did not find the tourists, but he did kill a guard and start a fire in the toolshed, leading Hector Raul to place a hefty bounty on Nary's head.

At this point in the book, Nary realizes the case was a sham and he is being hunted. He suspects the woman but does not know her motive or true identity. Nary tries to leave the country, but it's too late. Hector Raul has put people at the airport, bus stations, train stations, and the border crossings looking for the gringo. Now two parties want him dead.

Do you see any holes in the plot so far? Chet is disappointed Nary hasn't made any moves on any of the Bolivian women yet. I don't think this really

counts as a hole in the story. Mr. Nary really hasn't had the time. Chet says it seems impossible that someone as good-looking and confident as Chuck Nary hasn't kissed or even received a back rub from a native woman. If Chet represents the average consumer, I have to start taking his comments seriously.
Thanks,
Grady

- - - - - - - - - - - - - - - - - - -

To: Grady Thoms
From: Mair Pearson
Re: Plot Points

Grady, I do see a few plot holes in your book. It seems impossible Chuck Nary does not know Bolivia is a landlocked country. Also, he goes on a mission to South America without really knowing the woman who gave him the tip? No face-to-face meeting?

However, Bill and I do not want you to change anything in your story. We like it the way it is. Just finish the book and we'll talk plot points later.
Mair

- - - - - - - - - - - - - - - - - - -

To: Bill Williams
Cc: Mair Pearson
From: Grady Thoms
Subject: Accountability

Bill and Mair, I must admit something. Yesterday, I only worked on *Mr. Nary* for about half an hour. The day before, I didn't write at all. I'm finding it tough to force myself to work on the book. I need accountability. That is why I have decided to keep a daily log which I'll submit to you at the end of each day. You have a possible investment in me, and I need to be fair to you. If I know you'll be scrutinizing my every move, I'll think twice before watching Season One of *Grimm* again.

Here is today's time card. I didn't write as much as I should have, but I did think about it more knowing Bill would be examining my level of commitment. You will notice that I did not write down what I did between two and three this afternoon. That's because, for the life of me, I can't remember what it is I did.

TUESDAY

8:00 a.m.	Woke up
8:50 a.m.	Got out of bed
9:00 a.m.	Breakfast: Jimmy Dean sausage & egg sandwich.
9:20 a.m.	Showered and dressed. While shaving, I nicked my chin and had to use the end of a Q-tip to stop the bleeding as I was out of Band-Aids and toilet paper.
9:40 a.m.	Used the restroom. Unfortunately, still out of toilet paper and had to use Q-tips again.
10:00 a.m.	Made a list of items I needed at the store—toilet paper, Q-tips (I was out now), fruit, vegetables, meat, and candy.
10:10 a.m.	Showered again.
10:30 a.m.	Worked on chapter 10 of my book. Thought of some really good visuals but had trouble putting it down on paper. I wrote about a page of stuff.
11:30 a.m.	Went for a walk and threw rocks at a tree stump. I found a good walking stick but it broke when I swung it at a light pole. On the way back to the apartment, I saw Jenny walking her pug. She gave me a funny look. I wonder if it was the Q-tip swab on my chin or if she noticed I missed a belt loop.
12:00 p.m.	Made a few sales calls. Jim Thorp from *Intensity in Tent City* has agreed to try our new line of camouflage tarps but is still reluctant to try the bear repellent I've been pushing. He doesn't like that it's made from real bear urine, but bears hate the smell of their own urine. That's a fact.
1:30 p.m.	Picked up a burger and fries at Carl's Jr. for lunch. I

washed it down with a strawberry Weight Watchers shake. They taste great and help you lose weight.

2:00–3:00 p.m.   ???

3:00 p.m.   Drove up to Portland to drop off some minicoolers at *Lonely Lowell's*, the outdoor store with supplies geared for those without friends but who still enjoy nature. Outside the store, I waved and told a police officer I appreciated him, which I learned is a good way for getting searched for marijuana downtown.

4:15 p.m.   Went to the grocery store to purchase items from my list. I alerted the manager when I saw a person in the express lane who appeared to have twelve items. The guy tried to argue that his three yogurts should count as one item. Yeah right, buddy! They let him go through with a warning.

5:00 p.m.   At this time, I was back home sitting at the computer and thinking of ideas for chapter 10 while playing Plants vs Zombies.

5:05 p.m.   Got to level 5 on Plants vs Zombies.

5:15 p.m.   Got to level 10 on Plants vs Zombies.

5:30 p.m.   Got to level 15 of Plants vs Zombies. It became difficult to focus on the book with so many zombies attacking.

5:40 p.m.   Chet called and said his friend Trevor asked him to be the godfather to his newborn son. Chet was trying to think of a polite way to say no. He's got a lot of stuff going on at work and doesn't want the added responsibilities. I recommended he tell Trevor he doesn't see himself hanging around for the long run. An estranged godfather is worse than no godfather at all.

6:00 p.m.   Got back to the computer and wrote a couple hundred more words.

6:45 p.m.   Dinner: microwaved a chicken potpie. It burned my tongue. I don't think I've ever had a potpie that didn't burn my mouth. After dinner, I fixed my belt and went for another walk but didn't see Jenny.

| 8:00 p.m. | Reread what I wrote today, worked on daily time card, and e-mailed Bill. |

Let me know if you have questions. If I remember what it is I did at two o'clock this afternoon, I'll be sure to let you know.

Thanks,

Grady

- - - - - - - - - - - - - - - - - - - -

To: Grady Thoms
From: Mair Pearson
Re: Accountability

Grady, time cards are not necessary. As interesting as this is, you do not need to e-mail us your daily schedules. We trust you.

You will get more work done if you eliminate the distractions around your work area. Turn off your phone and resist the urge to play games. Continue to work on the book at the same time each day as part of your routine. Also, it might do you some good to see a nutritionist.

Mair

- - - - - - - - - - - - - - - - - - - -

To: Bill Williams
Cc: Mair Pearson
From: Grady Thoms
Subject: Car Chase Chapter

Bill and Mair, after struggling to stay on task, I've finally completed the epic car chase in chapter 10. I had some difficulty putting into words the grand spectacle pictured in my head. Writers do not have the luxury of CGI (computer generated imagery). We are stuck with having to describe stuff. It's still pretty action-packed, though. Forty-seven bystanders die, hundreds are injured, and thousands more are left homeless. I use the phrase "*insane fiery ball of flames*" three times. One of the highlights is when a train carrying angry bovines derails and sets loose the animals in a neighborhood where mostly old people reside.

The chase begins in the mountains near La Paz, as a distraught Chuck Nary returns to the orphanage to drop off Pey and the van. He notices a black SUV tailing him, and the hot pursuit begins. During fourteen pages of non-stop action, the chase teeters along perilous mountain roads, rumbles through miles of road construction, and accelerates into downtown where the *Dia Del Mar* parade is being staged. The assassins chasing Nary lose control of the SUV and die in an insane fiery collision with a whale-shaped float. It is wicked. Unfortunately, the orphanage van is totaled, and Mr. Nary is uninsured.

I don't really need your assistance with chapter 10, just letting you know it will not disappoint.

Thanks,

Grady

- - - - - - - - - - - - - - - - - -

To: Grady Thoms
From: Mair Pearson
Re: Car Chase Chapter

Grady, by all means, send chapter 10 our way. There are people in the office very eager to read it.

Mair

- - - - - - - - - - - - - - - - - -

To: Bill Williams
Cc: Mair Pearson
From: Grady Thoms
Subject: The Forward

Bill and Mair, Chet has offered to write the forward for Mr. Nary. If the purpose of the forward is to introduce the author to the reader and endorse the book, I can't think of anyone who could do that as well as Chet. Be warned, it gets a little wordy toward the end. He had a thesaurus on his lap when he wrote it. I think he is trying to impress you.

FORWARD

Ladies, Gentlemen, and people of the future reading this on your 3-D Kindles, I give you Grady Thoms. I first met this affable fellow in the fourth grade when my family moved to Oregon from Arizona to help alleviate my brother's allergies to petrified wood. I promptly learned that Grady was the kid to see if you were looking for a rare Garbage Pail Kid card or needed an impeccably made Chinese star. He was the only kid in school who could get you an authentic-looking bag of vomit in just a couple hours' notice.

Grady has had to overcome some adversities. In junior high, he was one of two boys in Clackamas County to famously lose a wrestling match to Mindy Welky. You may remember her on a segment on *60 Minutes,* which did a story on girls meddling in the affairs of men. During one clip, you can see Mindy execute a shrewd reversal on Grady, whose face was mercifully blurred by the show's producers.

In his junior year of high school, Grady ran for class president but came in a distant fourth place. Despite an aggressive campaign of pun-filled posters and promises of a longer lunch period with a salad bar, Grady received just seven votes. This was far less than the elected Mark Hawes, Debbie Anders, and even "Bull" from *Night Court,* who eleven people wrote in on their ballot as a joke. Some people might call these occurrences failures. I call them building blocks of a man.

Even though Grady has experienced a few minor setbacks, his disposition has remained buoyant. He does not give up. His ambitions do not retire. Grady Thoms is a consummate blend of persistence meeting ingenuity. A classic example is that he kept a neck brace in his locker to wear occasionally to gain sympathy from girls and teachers. The tactic worked well until the brace adopted an unpleasant odor. Undiscouraged, Grady switched his prop to crutches. It was a stroke of brilliance. After puppies, crutches are the second best way to have a girl approach you. Sure, everyone knows this now, but Grady was the pioneer.

In conclusion, I implore you to buy this book and embrace the odyssey of *Mr. Nary*, a character so undaunted it may transport you to mythical times when the lines of gods and men merged, yet remained apart. The tale you are about to embark upon exceeds acceptability, transcends quality, and is of the upmost coherence.

Chet Jensen

Mair, what do you think? At first, I didn't want Chet to mention Mindy Welky or my failed campaign for class president, but Chet says it gives me a certain amount of admirable vulnerability. He says people often mention the failures of the greats. Michael Jordan has missed over 9,000 shots. Babe Ruth struck out 1,330 times. Even Benjamin Franklin, one of the greatest presidents of all time, never graduated from high school.

Thanks,

Grady

- - - - - - - - - - - - - - - - - - -

To: Grady Thoms
From: Mair Pearson
Re: The Forward

Grady, here are a few facts about "forewords": they are commonly misspelled, they are written after the book is completed, and they are rarely used in fiction. Since nothing about you or your book is conventional, I say use the foreword. It was a big hit in the office.

Tell Chet that was impressive. He certainly has a commanding grasp of the English language. I did not even understand what he was carrying on about in the last paragraph (and I'm an English major).

Mair

- - - - - - - - - - - - - - - - - - -

To: Bill Williams
Cc: Mair Pearson
From: Grady Thoms
Subject: Chapter 11

Bill, I'm wondering if it's possible to skip chapter 11 and go straight to 12. The title could conjure up terrible memories over a bad business deal between my dad and my Uncle Craig when they had to file for chapter 11 bankruptcy. Several years ago, they started a line of expensive hand lotions strictly for blue-collar working men—farmers, plumbers, archeologists, etc. Unfortunately, the product never took off, and my dad blames Craig over the name, *Craig's Man Lotion for Men,* as the reason it failed. He lost most of his retirement and has never fully forgiven Uncle Craig. I just don't want my father to be reading the book and come to chapter 11 and say something like, "Chapter 11, huh…ask your uncle about that." He's still pretty snarky about it.

I thought it might not be that big of a deal to skip a chapter heading because, as you know, some hotels don't have a floor 13. The number is considered unlucky. I, too, am somewhat superstitious and try to avoid 13. If it's no big deal, I would like to skip 13 as well. So my chapters would go from chapter 10 to chapter 12 to chapter 14. If skipping two chapters is too much, omitting chapter 11 is my first choice.

I'm just glad this book's not going to reach anywhere close to 666 pages.
Thanks,
Grady

- - - - - - - - - - - - - - - - - - - -

To: Grady Thoms
From: Mair Pearson
Re: Chapter 11

Grady, it is nice of you to think of your father, but skipping a chapter is not a good idea. Readers will think they have a defective copy of your book and try to return it. One option is you could take the word "chapter" out and simply call it 11.
Mair

To: Bill Williams
Cc: Mair Pearson
From: Grady Thoms
Subject: A Poem for Jenny

Mair, you might be interested to know I had a five-minute conversation with Jenny yesterday. She says it's "really neat" that I'm writing a novel. She asked to read it, but I'm a little hesitant to give her unfinished work.

Bill, I told her *The Missionary* is very similar to *Mr. Nary.* I'm going to loan her my copy of your book to read. To let her know that you and I are friends, I signed and dedicated it from you. I hope that's okay. It's not really forgery because I'm not trying to sell it. I feel like if we ever meet face-to-face, you would sign the book anyway.

In case you meet Jenny someday (like at our wedding) and she asks about it, this is what you wrote: "*Grady, what can I say, you are a true friend. It has been an absolute pleasure to help you with your novel, Mr. Nary. Remember, a redwood tree starts out as a small acorn, and you, my friend, are an acorn. Also, thanks again for bailing me out with that one thing, I owe you big time. To another kindred soul—Bill.*"

I know this may sound as if we are closer than we really are but just give it time. This is how close I picture us someday.

As it turns out, Jenny loves to compose poetry. She likes to read and write about dark subjects such as death, global recession, and something she called unrequired love. She talked about it for a while but I had a hard time listening as I was trying to look natural as she spoke. My cousin Jesse says I have a tendency to get rigid when talking to girls.

Later, I wrote some of my own poetry and dedicated it to her. I'm thinking about giving it to her. It's called beginnings.

Beginnings

Her eyes, like thieves in a broken sun, forever and ever
Her lips, lonely and slightly chapped, so perfectly pink
It's quiet, so quiet

*His thoughts, unending electricity, like a dam holding back seethes of
passion building for a fortnight
His shoulders, strong but dormant, like cannons left over from a war,
a war no more
It's so quiet, so very quiet*

*Two paths cross under a desert moon, converging and merging into one
Down it goes, through violent storms, but they hold hands, make plans
Wolves in the distance dine on a fallen caribou; yet she feels safe
Still quiet, so…so quiet*

Jenny, would you like to have dinner? It's Grady, from upstairs.

I'm thinking about slipping this under her door tonight. What do you think?
Thanks,
Grady

- - - - - - - - - - - - - - - - - - - -

To: Grady Thoms
From: Mair Pearson
Re: A Poem for Jenny

Grady, good grief. How did I get from your literary aid to giving you dating
advice? I am glad you asked my opinion, however, and I pray for your sake
that I am not too late. Do not slide that poem under her door. It is too much,
too forward, and a little scary. This is the behavior of stalkers. It is bad
enough that you falsely dedicated the book from Bill.

If you want to ask her out, casually ask her out for a cup of coffee or a
drink. Bring a friend along and allow her to bring one too. Don't be too persistent, give her room (you are not selling camping equipment). Then rip up
that note and burn it. Continue to work on *Mr. Nary*. Stay focused, no more
poetry. This is a direct order from Bill.
Mair

- - - - - - - - - - - - - - - - - - - -

To: Bill Williams
Cc: Mair Pearson
From: Grady Thoms
Subject: Bet with Chet

Mair, it's too late, I slipped the poem under her door late last night. I wished you had e-mailed me sooner as I'm feeling some morning regret. It's funny how the light of day can put a spotlight on your shame. I should stop making decisions when I'm tired.

The good news is that if she does accept my date proposal, I should have some extra cash. Chet is betting me twenty dollars I can't fit in the phrase "*This isn't women's soccer*" in my manuscript. I think I can do it. It will have to be used in dialogue, as it would be silly for the narrator to say something like that. I could have Chuck Nary say it after Pubano asks him if this case reminds him of women's soccer. And Nary will say, "*No, Pubano, this isn't women's soccer.*"

It will be our little joke, and the reader won't even know it's out of place. This will be the easiest twenty dollars I ever made.
Thanks,
Grady

- - - - - - - - - - - - - - - - - - -

To: Grady Thoms
From: Mair Pearson
Re: Bet with Chet

Grady, I have no response to this.
Mair

- - - - - - - - - - - - - - - - - - -

To: Mair Pearson
From: Grady Thoms
Subject: Women's Fan Club

Mair, I am wondering if you would be interested in being the chairman of my new fan club for women, Grady's Ladies. Basically, it would be an online chat room where women could talk about my book and maybe swap recipes or share tips on removing stains.

I picture the front page of the site to be a cozy yet feminine living room with Victorian furniture, flowers, and virtual tea. Maybe we could play female-friendly tunes by Josh Groban or Phil Collins. Once at the site, a Grady Lady can enter one of the chat rooms, depending on what she wants to talk about. When four or more enter a room, the chat begins. Each room would have a designated person policing the conversation in case the others get off subject (my book) for too long.

As the chairwoman of Grady's Ladies, your duties would not be much. You just need to make sure passwords are working and the site is not being infiltrated by rival fan clubs. Once a year, you could lead a Grady Thoms field trip in Wilsonville, where you drive a bus and show the women my elementary school, my apartment, and the Chili's restaurant where I first drew a picture of Chuck Nary on a napkin.

Do you think we should charge a monthly service fee for this? I'm leaning toward no fees because Grady's Ladies are my diehard fans. They bought my book and stood in long lines to get it signed. The website can wait until the book is published of course, so don't worry about the costs to construct gradysladies.com. We will let *Mr. Nary* generate some capital first. Just have some templates ready.

I attached a sign-up sheet the lady fans can fill out online or by mail. Let's start compiling a master list.

GRADY'S LADIES FAN CLUB

NAME_____ E-mail_____

Nickname (example—Tina)_____

Work E-mail _____ Other E-mail _____

Cell Phone # _____ Home Phone # _____

Work Phone #_____ Fax Number # _____

Pager # _____ Emergency Contact # _____

Sister's Phone # _____ Best Friend's # _____

Mother's Phone # (Optional) _____

Where You Live _____

What You Drive_____ License Plate # _____

Where You Work Out _____

What You Do _____

(Check one) ____ I want daily updates ____ I want weekly updates

What did you think of my book? __ Good __ Great __ Absolutely loved it

Do You like Animals? Yes No

Signature _____ Date _____

Congratulations, you are now a member of Grady's Ladies, an exclusive club for all women. As a Grady Lady, you will be given a username (like SisterNary) and a password to gradiesladies.com, where you can chat with other female Mr. Nary fans about the book, the author, and what it's like having babies. We will keep you updated on field trips and future book signings.

Looking forward to hearing from you,
Grady

- - - - - - - - - - - - - - - - - - - -

To: Grady Thoms
From: Mair Pearson
Re: Women's Fan Club

Grady, fan clubs are usually started by fans and run by those fans. The chairman of your club must also be "a fan". Since I am not really a fan, I must respectfully decline. Sorry. :(

Maybe you could ask Jenny from your apartment to run the club. It could be relationship suicide, but you never know. Have you asked her out for coffee yet? I am curious what she thought of your poem.

By the way, I did some quick research on gradysladies.com, and unfortunately, it is taken. It appears the female fans of the Cleveland Indian outfielder Grady Sizemore beat you to the punch. If your next question is what legal action we can take against them, the answer is none.
Mair

- - - - - - - - - - - - - - - - - - -

To: Mair Pearson
From: Grady Thoms
Re: Women's Fan Club

Mair, thanks for doing the research. As you know, I just don't have the time. What about Ladies4Grady.com? Any of the following domain names will work. In fact, Grady's Ladies could be broken down into subgroups:

GradysSexySadies.com (fans of The Beatles and my book)
GradyThomsLadyMoms.com (for the mothers)
ChuckNaryAndTheVirginMary.com (Catholic fans of my book)
WomenWhoLikeMrNary.com (for those not into rhyming fan clubs)

The options are limitless.

No, I have not asked Jenny out yet. We've chatted a few times, and I've left notes on her car saying I hope she has an awesome day of work at the hair salon. I'm building a friend foundation. She must have liked my poem because she slipped one of her own under my door the other day. It was about how she will never go fishing with her favorite uncle again because he's dead. She is very deep.

Thanks,

Grady

- - - - - - - - - - - - - - - - - - -

To: Bill Williams
Cc: Mair Pearson
From: Grady Thoms
Subject: The Albino Spy

Bill and Mair, the action continues in chapter 12 as Chuck Nary takes out another spy in the busy streets of Centro. Nary catches on to a man trailing him, an albino with a severe sunburn, and doubles back to confront him. The spy, realizing his cover is blown, turns to run. Mr. Nary grabs a papaya from a fruit stand and hurls it high in the air toward him. The heavy fruit strikes the albino in the head, causing him to fall on his own dagger, piercing his spleen while spilling his 60 SPF sunscreen all over the sidewalk. The man is able to gurgle a few bloody words to Nary before exhaling his last breath—"*La mujer te le traiciono*" (the woman betrayed you).

The reason I made the spy an albino is that I'm trying to make each character stand out. I was going to give him a beard as well, but Chet says albinos can't grow beards. Have you heard of this? Chet also claims that there are no Native American midgets. I think he has this backwards. I think Native Americans can't grow beards and there are no albino midgets. Sometimes I can't believe the things Chet says. In junior high, he told me his dad invented the sports bra.

The deaths are mounting in Bolivia. This story is taking a more menacing tone then I imagined.

Thanks,

Grady

- - - - - - - - - - - - - - - - - - -

To: Grady Thoms
From: Mair Pearson
Re: The Albino Spy

Grady, you might be able to offend every race, social class, and ethnic group by the time your book is finished. I implore you, if you ever decide to include little people (the preferred term) in your book, do not use the word "midget" in the narrative. It is considered derogatory. I noticed you used the correct term for Native Americans, but not for little people. Interesting.

Regarding the spy, I would think undercover work would be an unlikely vocation for an albino, especially if you need to be incognito in South America. If I had to hire a spy in Bolivia, I would go local. However, Bill and I agree he suits this particular story.
Mair

- - - - - - - - - - - - - - - - - - -

To: Mair Pearson
From: Grady Thoms
Re: The Albino Spy

Mair, I've heard the term "little people" but did not know it was what they preferred to be called. I will retire "midget" from my vocabulary. I guess it's like when people use demeaning terms to describe camping gear salesmen, like wood nerds, cooler rats, or forest lickers.

I was not going to have any little people in my book anyway, except for maybe a quick scene when Mr. Nary and Pubano stumble upon an urban pickup basketball game played and officiated entirely by little people.
Thanks,
Grady

- - - - - - - - - - - - - - - - - - -

To: Mair Pearson
Cc: Bill Williams
From: Grady Thoms
Subject: My Birthday

Bill and Mair, today is my birthday, so I will not be working on my book. I'm sure you understand. My birthday celebrations tend to be pretty memorable. My cousin Jesse usually has something up his sleeve—long hikes, canoeing lessons, baking contests, etc. One time he hired a horticulturist and we spent the entire day in the woods identifying trees. It was pretty sweet.

For dinner, I'm going to drive over to my dad's place for some smoked venison he prepared. Last week, he hit a doe with his truck and is going to have a head-mounting ceremony in the garage. This will be his sixth deer head on the wall. People think he's a great hunter or something, but he's actually hit all of them with his truck. Sometimes I think he just drives his old Ford pickup around the back roads late at night trying to hit deer. He even has a little fawn head mounted. My dad says it's okay because it was an "accident." During Christmas, he brings the heads into the living room and gives them reindeer names. He needs two more to complete his collection. People love his Christmas parties. He makes great eggnog.

After dinner, I plan to meet up with Chet at McMenamins for Cajun tots and a couple of black raspberry lemonades over a game of cribbage. Don't wait up for me.

Thanks,

Grady

- - - - - - - - - - - - - - - - - - -

To: Grady Thoms
From: Mair Pearson
Re: My Birthday

Happy Birthday, Grady. Unlike most writers, it sounds like you know how to paint the town red.
Mair

- - - - - - - - - - - - - - - - - - -

To: Bill Williams
Cc: Mair Pearson
From: Grady Thoms
Subject: Adjectives

Bill and Mair, I'm running out of good adjectives. I've heard adjectives are the seasonings of a tasty story and it's a good idea to sprinkle them in liberally. I want solid descriptions but fear I'm overusing the best ones. How many times can I use the same adjective to describe a noun? In one passage, I use *powerful* three times: "*It was a powerful jump,*" "*It was a powerful leg whip,*" and "*It was a powerful moment between two powerful warriors under the city lights.*"

Thanks,

Grady

- - - - - - - - - - - - - - - - - -

To: Grady Thoms
From: Mair Pearson
Re: Adjectives

Grady, by my count, you used *powerful* four times. Powerful is okay, but the real effective words are nouns and verbs. Verbs show action. And choosing the right word is what good writing is all about. One word can make or break an entire paragraph. It can resonate with the reader long after it is used.

Find a thesaurus online and punch in the word you would like to substitute. You will see over forty alternatives for powerful, for example. Play with different words and read each one aloud in the sentence. Most of the time, you will eventually hear the word you are looking for.

Mair

- - - - - - - - - - - - - - - - - -

To: Bill Williams
Cc: Mair Pearson
From: Grady Thoms
Subject: Unexpected Death

Bill and Mair, I am sad to announce that Pey, the mute orphan, is dead. Toward the end of chapter 12, he is caught in the middle of exchanged gunfire between Chuck Nary, Pubano, and the drug cartel. Nary and Pubano are okay, but the young boy is taken down by a stray bullet. This makes Mr.

Nary extremely upset. The kid became his friend. He taught Nary how to play Spanish checkers and did not judge him for having a cold sore. Nary confided secrets to Pey, like his fear of snorkeling and how he rarely used the sanitary toilet-seat covers at gas station restrooms because he figured everyone else did so he didn't need to.

Chuck Nary holds the dying boy in his arms and tells Pey, "*Death visits all our doors, and he will visit the door of the ones who did this to you tomorrow or maybe the next day. I promise you that!*" At that moment, Pey thought his last words and drifted off to sleep.

I am sad Pey died. I did not intend for this to happen. It just did. The story is really taking a life of its own. Sometimes I feel as if a voice outside my head is telling me what to write. I just listen and type. I really hope Pubano lives, he is my favorite character.

Things are heating up. I just wanted to keep you in the loop of what's going on. I know publishers can get antsy when they haven't heard from their writers in awhile. Don't worry, I'm hard at work.
Thanks,
Grady

- - - - - - - - - - - - - - - - - - -

To: Grady Thoms
From: Mair Pearson
Re: Unexpected Death

Grady, it is good you feel sad about the death of Pey. It shows that you care about your characters. If the writer cares about them, your reader will too. By the way, you never told us what the initials stood for in his name.
Mair

- - - - - - - - - - - - - - - - - - -

To: Mair Pearson
From: Grady Thoms
Re: Unexpected Death

Mair, the letters in PEY originally stood for "Protect Earth's Young," but since Pey died and Mr. Nary failed to keep him safe, I feel a little ashamed to mention it in the book. Let's just keep this between us. If people ask, we can say PEY stands for "Please Enjoy Your..." And if they ask "Please enjoy your...what?" We can just say, "Well...that's what we all have to ask ourselves, isn't it?" And then we should walk away from the conversation.

Thanks,

Grady

- - - - - - - - - - - - - - - - - - -

To: Mair Pearson
Cc: Bill Williams
From: Grady Thoms
Subject: Female Lead

Mair, Chet's wife said my book is destined for failure because I don't have a strong female lead. She says I might as well write about manatees because that's how much I know about grown women. I laughed in her face because I know a lot about manatees. Unfortunately, she's right about women. I'm still working up the nerve to ask out Jenny from my apartment.

I do have the character Sophia, the evil woman with the grudge against Nary, but she has a small part. The only other female character is Pubano's wife, Alegria. I suppose I could give her a more central role. I could talk more about her cooking, cleaning, and gentle nagging she gives Pubano. That should appease my women readers.

How important is it that I appeal to women in my book?

Thanks,

Grady

- - - - - - - - - - - - - - - - - - -

To: Grady Thoms
From: Mair Pearson
Re: Female Lead

Grady, your book does not and should not have to appeal to women. You

are writing about the struggles of men from a man's point of view. Not everyone is going to enjoy the book. Some will hate it. That's okay. It is best to keep it centered in bravado, staying true to your characters and your abilities. While I personally find your style odd, many in the office continue to enjoy your entries. Keep writing!
Mair

- - - - - - - - - - - - - - - - - - -

To: Mair Pearson
Cc: Bill Williams
From: Grady Thoms
Subject: New Writer's Club in Town

Mair, I've decided to start my own writer's group. I bet there are other writers out there looking for community. Anyone with a passion for writing can be a part of the group. All genres (but not erotic) are welcomed—political thrillers, romantic comedies, teenage angst, old-people hobbies, and even cookbooks. What do you think we should call our group? I like *BRAG* (Beginning wRiters Are Great).

So far, there are three of us in the club—myself, Jenny, and Chet. As you know, Jenny writes poetry and is excited to be in an interactive group. This should provide me the opportunity to ask her out. As you know, Chet also writes and has many interesting things to say. He is a prolific user on Yelp and has written over five hundred reviews. Chet is the only person I know who has written a review for a mortuary. He gave Valley Crest Funeral Home three stars.

Shane, a warehouse worker at *Intensity in Tent City,* is also interested in joining the club. He wants us to help him write letters to Congress. It is Shane's goal to make it legal to fish the Willamette River with M80s during certain times of the year—as long as you're a descendant of the tribe (he is one-eighth Chinook). He also wants the freedom to own a flamethrower for recreational use in the state of Oregon for those with one strike or less on their record. His ideas are a little out there but if Shane joins, we would have enough to start meeting. I would like six to eight members, but I don't know anyone else who writes. I created an ad on Craigslist. So far, no one has responded. I pasted it below so you could look at it and tell me if I need to add anything to it.

Title: BRAG Writing Group to Meet in my Apartment (please bring your own chair)

Body: Are you the next Ernest Hemmingway, Salmon Rushdie, or Anne Frank? We want you in BRAG! (Beginning wRiters Are Great.) All writing styles welcome! We will be meeting Tuesdays at my apartment at 7 p.m. So far, there are three of us in the group. The other two will not be able to make all of the meetings, so sometimes it will just be you and me. I do have a small couch, so on those days you will not need to bring a chair, although that seating arrangement is difficult to face each other. If you prefer to have eye contact, we can go sit on my waterbed. Also, do you like Red Vines? I do!

Mair, should I say anything else?

Thanks,

Grady

- - - - - - - - - - - - - - - - - - - -

To: Grady Thoms
From: Mair Pearson
Re: New Writer's Club in Town

Grady, I can see why no one has responded to your ad. It is rather off-putting. If you want people to respond, I would cut the ad after you mention the time and place.
Mair

- - - - - - - - - - - - - - - - - - - -

To: Mair Pearson
From: Grady Thoms
Re: New Writer's Club in Town

Mair, what is "off-putting"? I've heard people say that before. The other day,

someone told me my cologne was "off-putting." Is that like tapioca putting?
If so, I don't mind.
Thanks,
Grady

April

To: Mair Pearson
Cc: Bill Williams
From: Grady Thoms
Subject: Lost Control

Mair, I'm losing control of Chuck Nary. As I get deeper into the story and the danger grows around him, he is forced to do awful things to survive. Did I tell you about the jungle scene where he eats a monkey he befriended? It gets worse. Nary decides to go on a rampage for the death of Pey. He buys a crossbow, paints war stripes on his face, and goes to the private residence of Hector Raul. Once there, Nary takes off his shirt and lights it on fire in the driveway, yelling for Hector to come out and fight like a man. An older gentleman steps out to tell him he has the wrong house. Nary leaves without apologizing.

Later, Mr. Nary is walking through a park downtown when he kicks a pigeon that is late in getting out of the way. The pigeon doesn't die but can no longer fly straight. His bitterness has turned him into a ruffian. He begins shouting at passing tourists that Bolivia is not worth visiting because it has no coast. He starts calling it *South America's Oklahoma*.

I don't know what I'm going to do. Chuck Nary is not acting like a hero. He's turning into a villain. He's gone completely rogue and no longer trusts anyone, not even Pubano. Worst of all, Mr. Nary is acting on his own. How do I get control of him again?
Thanks,
Grady

- - - - - - - - - - - - - - - - - - -

To: Grady Thoms
From: Mair Pearson
Re: Lost Control

Grady, I am not sure what to say. I find it hard to believe that you are losing your protagonist. I say let him go, let's see what happens. It is good he is making the decisions. I am sure he will come back. Please keep me updated on his progress. Everyone at BWA is interested in what happens next.

By the way, Chuck Nary eating a monkey is pretty dark, Grady. Even for you.
Mair

- - - - - - - - - - - - - - - - - - -

To: Mair Pearson
From: Grady Thoms
Re: Lost Control

Mair, don't worry about the monkey. It's not one of those monkeys with a lot of personality, like in the movie *Project X*. This monkey is one of those disease-infested screeching monkeys that tries to give you a poisoned date, like in *Indiana Jones*.
Thanks,
Grady

- - - - - - - - - - - - - - - - - - -

To: Mair Pearson
Cc: Bill Williams
From: Grady Thoms
Subject: Torture Scene

Mair, Chuck Nary has captured Jabby, the mid-level drug runner, and is holding him hostage in an abandoned garage. He plans to retrieve information using various torture tactics. At first, Nary starts slowly by plucking out hairs from his beard and eyebrows using rusty tweezers. When that doesn't work, he begins to yell loudly in his ears. Yet Jabby holds strong. Things are about to get worse. I can feel it. I'm really afraid of what Nary is going to do next. Nary leaves the garage to find some jumper cables and a pair of dull sheep shears for the torture. I stopped writing because I don't have control of where Nary will take it next. I was hoping Jabby would cave in after the yelling, but he did not.

To make matters worse, I've been having nightmares. In my last dream, Chuck Nary was driving a bus with me and a couple of my clients in the back. He veers off the highway to take us on a narrow shortcut through some woods. As the light is fading, he maneuvers us down a jarring path cramped with overgrown blackberry bushes. The dirt road deteriorates into mud and eventually becomes a stream. We keep sloshing on. My clients are hysterical and Mr. Nary is yelling—then negotiating with someone outside our realm. The stream is now a river. The bus teeters along and picks up speed. Then I woke up.

Do you think this dream has more to do with Chuck Nary or my clients, who have been complaining over the increased prices of survival chili and dehydrated stew? Maybe it's time to sell my waterbed. I'm sick of river-themed dreams (and going to the chiropractor to get my back fixed). Other times I wake up anxious and don't remember the dream, but I'm sure it involves Mr. Nary. What should I do with him?

Thanks,

Grady

- - - - - - - - - - - - - - - - - - -

To: Grady Thoms
From: Mair Pearson
Re: Torture Scene

Grady, I think you are beginning to mix your reality with your fiction. You may need to look into speaking with a local psychologist to help you gain insight.

Chuck Nary is your character. You created him, and no one knows him like you do. Get behind his eyes and try to understand why he is behaving in this manner. Using this information, shape his actions using his strengths. But remember, do not go out of character.

Mair

- - - - - - - - - - - - - - - - - - -

To: Mair Pearson
From: Grady Thoms
Re: Torture Scene

Mair, I looked for a psychic online as you suggested and found one called "Serenity by Sarah." She does intuitive and palm readings. Maybe she will

do political thriller readings as well? If she does readings, maybe she would like to join BRAG. You think she can help me gain control of Chuck Nary?
Thanks,
Grady

- - - - - - - - - - - - - - - - - -

To: Grady Thoms
From: Mair Pearson
Re: Torture Scene

Grady, you have the habit of misreading and misinterpreting my e-mails. A psychologist is a licensed professional who helps people with their mental health, like Lorraine Bracco from *The Sopranos*. A psychic is a person who, for forty dollars, will tell you that your book will become a best seller. You do not want to consult one of those.
Mair

- - - - - - - - - - - - - - - - - -

To: Mair Pearson
Cc: Bill Williams
From: Grady Thoms
Subject: Psychologist

Mair, do you think it's possible to create a psychologist to talk to Chuck Nary? I could say he's an English doctor in La Paz on holiday. He sees Nary walking down the street and immediately recognizes this man needs help. I may need to contact a real psychologist for research and to help with the dialogue. He could guide me on what the psychologist would say to Mr. Nary. Let's give him a smart name like Dr. Henry Watson III. I'll start looking for one in the online phone book.
Thanks,
Grady

- - - - - - - - - - - - - - - - - -

To: Grady Thoms
From: Mair Pearson
Re: Psychologist

Grady, as long as you talk to a psychologist, whether it is for your character or for you, it should help. People here are curious to see how your search for a doctor goes, especially Bill. Please keep us updated.
Mair

- - - - - - - - - - - - - - - - - - -

To: Mair Pearson
Cc: Bill Williams
From: Grady Thoms
Re: Psychologist

Mair, I reached out to a Dr. Richard Logan and explained my situation. He had the gall to say I might be the one who needed counseling, not my character. Yeah right, Dr. Logan. Chuck Nary is the one who befriended and ate the monkey, not me. He hung up when I told him he was a pretend doctor who heals only imaginary problems. Being the bigger man, I called back to say I was sorry for calling his profession a joke and I respected his opinion. He accepted my apology and convinced me to set up an appointment for this morning. I didn't bother to show up, though.

I guess I will have to learn psychology myself. Chet says I can get a degree in ten days on the Internet, but I am skeptical of Chet's claims. He still swears to this day he coined the popular phrase, "Don't be talkin' jive turkey."

Otherwise, I'll have to find a new solution to gain control of Chuck Nary, who is just a few pages away from blowing up a bridge.
Thanks,
Grady

- - - - - - - - - - - - - - - - - - -

To: Mair Pearson
Cc: Bill Williams
From: Grady Thoms
Subject: Torture Scene Avoided

Mair, we got lucky. While Chuck Nary was out looking for sheep shears, thumb-screws, and kosher salt, Jabby the drug dealer was able to loosen his ropes and escape. Seeing he was gone, Mr. Nary goes ballistic. He throws a wooden chair against the wall and goes into a profanity-laced tirade that would make a municipal golf pro blush. I don't remember Chuck Nary having such a bad temper when I created his character profile. The death of Pey has really affected him.
Thanks,
Grady

- - - - - - - - - - - - - - - - - - -

To: Grady Thoms
From: Mair Pearson
Re: Torture Scene Avoided

Grady, that was a close call, although I am a little curious what Mr. Nary was going to do with sheep shears and kosher salt.
Mair

- - - - - - - - - - - - - - - - - - -

To: Mair Pearson
Cc: Bill Williams
From: Grady Thoms
Subject: Chuck Nary's Drinking Problem

Mair, Chuck Nary is turning into a drunk. He went into a bar and proceeded to drink an entire six-pack of beer in less than an hour. Consequently, he passes out on the floor and has to be carried out to the street, where he is left for dead. A Good Samaritan takes pity on him and delivers Nary to a local hospital to get his stomach pumped.

Once Mr. Nary is released, he proceeds to go to another bar and drink two more dark beers. Now drunk again, Chuck Nary starts asking around where he can go bet on some cockfighting. The bartender tells him there is no cockfighting on Sundays, so Nary throws his boots at a painting of the Bolivian president hanging above the bar and storms out.

Now that Nary realizes there is no cruise ship or missing couple, he has fallen into a deep depression. He wants revenge for the death of Pey, yet he finds himself seeking the constant three-beer buzz. It's foolishness. If he continues to drink at this pace, he's going to wake up with Jim Blossoms on his face.

Meanwhile, the dangers continue to grow around Chuck Nary. Hector Raul has put a bounty on his head. Sophia's hired assassins are ready to take him out at a moment's notice. Government officials have been ordered to detain him for ruining the best Dia del Mar parade since 1992. Yet despite all this, he has become his own worst enemy.

Thanks,
Grady

- - - - - - - - - - - - - - - - - - -

To: Grady Thoms
From: Mair Pearson
Re: Chuck Nary's Drinking Problem

Grady, how much does Chuck Nary weigh—eighty pounds? I find it hard to believe he would need his stomach pumped after a few beers. Did you create a psychiatrist to talk to Chuck Nary? I think that could have been an interesting angle.
Mair

- - - - - - - - - - - - - - - - - - -

To: Mair Pearson
From: Grady Thoms
Re: Chuck Nary's Drinking Problem

Mair, what is the difference between a psychologist and a psychiatrist? Aren't they the same? And what does a therapist do? Or a counselor? There are too many labels in that field. I think it's a ploy by them to make us more crazy and drum up some business.

I have decided against writing in a "psychiatrist" to help Chuck Nary. I don't want to bog the story down with a bunch of doctor/patient talking sessions, even though it could help Nary. This is a political thriller, not the Barbra Streisand movie *Prince of Times*.

Thanks,

Grady

- - - - - - - - - - - - - - - - - - -

To: Mair Pearson
Cc: Bill Williams
From: Grady Thoms
Subject: A Drink with Jenny

Mair, you might be interested to know I took your advice and asked Jenny out for coffee last night. She thought it was too late for coffee but could go for a beer. I don't drink beer but said "a beer sounded really, really good." Sometimes I'll have an MHL (Mike's Hard Lemonade), but I rarely drink beer. I figured I might as well do some research if Chuck Nary is going to have a drinking problem. So we headed off to Murphy's Irish Pub down the street and each ordered a Guinness. Guinness may look like chocolate milk, but the taste is similar to chewing Advil. I know because I can't swallow pills.

When going on a first date, I like to bring a list of items to talk about so there is no uncomfortable silence. Topics range from my low body fat percentage to the fact that I'm an Oregon donor for the DMV. My cousin Jesse says to let the girl do most of the talking and avoid bringing up personal issues. In the past, I've made the mistake of asking my date if her family has a history of high blood pressure or if she bothers folding her bras. I suppose those are more of third- or fourth-date type inquiries.

Maybe it was the second Guinness, but I became relaxed with Jenny. I learned her dad is an orthodontist and a perfectionist. Jenny has had braces for twelve years now. Every checkup he tells her it will be just six more months. She thinks she might die with braces on. That's when I made my move and said, "I hope I'm there when you die." She asked me what I meant and I said, "You know, that we know each other that long until you die."

She thought that was sweet but said I might die first. That's highly unlikely, I told her, given my genetic history.

All in all, I would say it was a success. I was honest (except for telling her I like beer), and she didn't seem repulsed by anything I said. We agreed to hit Murphy's once a week for happy hour and talk about my book. I better acquire a taste for potato skins and Guinness, but that shouldn't be too hard. I could have easily drank another Guinness but I don't want to turn into Chuck Nary. Thanks,
Grady

- - - - - - - - - - - - - - - - - - -

To: Grady Thoms
From: Mair Pearson
Re: A Drink with Jenny

Grady, glad to hear the date went well. Hopefully, I am done giving you relationship advice and we can focus on your book.
Mair

- - - - - - - - - - - - - - - - - - -

To: Mair Pearson
Cc: Bill Williams
From: Grady Thoms
Subject: Alegria Gets Kidnapped

Mair, in chapter 14, Alegria got nabbed by a couple of Hector Raul's men while she was out shopping (I wrote a couple paragraphs about Alegria finding a dress on sale—sometimes I'll throw my female readers a bone). Pubano is desperate to find her because he loves her and she does all the baking at La Banana Chica.

Unfortunately, Chuck Nary is little help. He's depressed, mostly drunk, and living on the streets at the moment. Pubano is unable to find him. The good news is that Hector Raul can't either. Nary would be pretty easy to kill right now. He drinks his days away and stumbles from store to store looking for Stoker's Chewing Tobacco, which is only sold in Texas. At night, he cries over Pey's death and blames himself. He vowed a life of muteness like Pey, but it didn't last long as he asked a local man where he could find a chili dog.

I don't know what Pubano is going to do to get his wife back. Hector Raul sent a ransom note giving him an ultimatum. Pubano can either deliver two hundred thousand Bolivianos or hand over Chuck Nary in exchange for the release of Alegria. He has three days. After that, Alegria will be tied to a meat barrel and thrown into the Rio Los Dientes, a piranha-infested river. Pubano will never see her again, and the bakery will eventually suffer from bad reviews.

Pubano finds himself in an *el encurtido* (a pickle). He does not have the money or the resources to rescue his wife. He wants to stay loyal to his friend, but he needs Alegria back. Chuck Nary is the only one he knows who could pull off the rescue. Yet he is in no condition to save anyone.

Thanks,
Grady

- - - - - - - - - - - - - - - - - - -

To: Grady Thoms
From: Mair Pearson
Re: Alegria Gets Kidnapped

Grady, what is a meat barrel? Is it a barrel made of meat products? We have a bet going in the office.
Mair

- - - - - - - - - - - - - - - - - - -

To: Mair Pearson
From: Grady Thoms
Re: Alegria Gets Kidnapped

Mair, a meat barrel is a hollowed-out log. I made it up.
Thanks,
Grady

To: Mair Pearson
Cc: Bill Williams
From: Grady Thoms
Subject: New Character to Replace Chuck Nary

Mair, I'm bringing in a new character in chapter 15. His name is Chester Biggles. Chester will fly down to Bolivia and take the place of Chuck Nary as the protagonist. Using his smarts, he will help Pubano get his wife back. I'm going to make this new character a really nice guy. He will never lose his temper, get drunk, or become attached to orphans. I will make him much easier to control.

I've come to the conclusion that I need to kill off Chuck Nary. He has become too dangerous and unpredictable to keep alive. Perhaps I can give him a peaceful death, like dying of pneumonia or exposure. You're probably wondering how one dies from exposure. I will tell you. As an expert in wilderness survival, you need to be aware of the symptoms of exposure—cotton mouth, numbness of the extremities, hallucinations, and paranoia. I've heard it's a lot like being on mushrooms.

This is the paragraph I wrote if I decide to kill Mr. Nary of exposure:

Chuck Nary stumbled along the waterfront, his body numb and mind fuzzy from exposure. Dropping to the grass, Nary rolled to face the light blue sun, distant and frozen in the sky. The exposure had crept into his lungs now, time was short. He had lived a good life but mistakes were made. Above Nary, a swaying palo santo discarded its leaves without much thought, like an obese child shedding Tootsie Roll wrappers. He wondered when the tree would fall. His thoughts turned to his father, Robert Nary, whose endless lessons failed to mention the dangers of exposure. Chuck would never say good-bye to his mother. He pictured her draped in black garments, searching the country for his unmarked grave, grieving for closure. It would be Mr. Nary's last thought. The exposure crept over his body and skull like a warm blanket, yet he was completely exposed.

I know this is a bit morbid, but at least I could go on with the story.

Chester Biggles can carry on from here. I cannot believe it has come to this, but here we are. Mr. Nary, our flawed hero, will die.

Thanks,

Grady

- - - - - - - - - - - - - - - - - - - -

To: Grady Thoms
From: Mair Pearson
Re: New Character to Replace Chuck Nary

Grady, while every character has flaws, you want the reader to like the protagonist and hope for his ultimate success. I find it hard to believe the main character will die halfway through the book. Will you now change the title to *Mr. Biggles?*

Mair

- - - - - - - - - - - - - - - - - - - -

To: Mair Pearson
From: Grady Thoms
Re: New Character to Replace Chuck Nary

Mair, I will not be changing the name of the book. *Mr. Nary* is more about an idea or social commentary on foreign freedoms and intercultural injustices than an actual character. You can see it all in the multiple allegories I've laid out along the way.

Thanks,

Grady

- - - - - - - - - - - - - - - - - - - -

To: Mair Pearson
Cc: Bill Williams
From: Grady Thoms
Subject: Chester Biggles's Character Profile

Mair, here is Chester Biggles's profile. I think you are going to like him. He's very intelligent, calm, and focused. He will be able to stay on task and not fall victim to a quick temper or strong drink.

Chester Biggles Profile

Chester grew up in a prominent family in Hanover, New Hampshire. His father, Charles, a professor of Engineering Bio Medical Statistics of Improbable Mathematics at Dartmouth, never raised his voice at his three children. He rarely spoke but when he did, it was the sort of profound declaration a Fortune 500 company would use as a mission statement. The children always stopped what they were doing to listen. He would say things such as, "Let us not pledge a life of indifference, but rather, pledge a life of difference in." It was no wonder he was always asked to give the commencement speech.

Chester's mother Moonshay (pronounced moon-shay), a stay-at-home socialite, inherited an enormous amount of wealth and prestige from her father, Reginald Prixley, a pioneer in lobster farming. Moonshay threw lavish parties where the guests wore scarves made of fox tails, drank champagne, and spoke what little French they knew. Chester, the firstborn, was secretly her favorite. She liked Barbara too, the baby of the family. Bobby, the middle child, was okay.

Chester grew up smart and handsome, but you would never know he knew it by talking to him. He deflected questions about his 4.0 GPA, chiseled chin, and sandy hair by asking you about your interests. Every girl at the private institute of Millard Fillmore Academy loved Chester. It didn't hurt that he was three-year tennis champion.

Taking after his father, Chester was very frugal with his money. Before going on a date, he would have the girl sign an agreement stating he would buy her one entree and one drink, including tip. If his date wanted a second drink or a dessert, she would have to purchase the item herself. Surprisingly, young girls found dating agreements extremely sexy. It's when the women get older that these "prenuptials" start to lose their flavor.

Chester could have chosen any career and been successful. His passion was helping people, especially kidnapped victims. Chester wanted to start an organization dedicated to looking for missing people. He got the idea on a date while watching the movie Ransom, where he paid for the girl's movie ticket but not her popcorn.

Three years later, People Napped Organization opened shop in Boston. Their motto was "People napped, because it's not just kids." Chester, the founder and the president, only received payment if the missing person was located (half-price if the missing person was found dead). Chester relied on his intelligence and connections to find people. Rarely was he involved in any altercations. If it was too dangerous, he would contact the police.

When Pubano called his office, Chester could barely understand the strange Bolivian, something about his wife being kidnapped and his drunk friend not helping. Chester thought about sending his partner Collin to Bolivia, but ultimately decided to take the case. He always wanted to visit a country where Speedos and bronze medallions were socially acceptable. Besides, he had no wife or kids holding him down. Chester took down Pubano's information and began looking for flights.

Chester's Weaknesses: Dry skin, thin lips, does not look great in a pair of jeans, uses both hands while eating with chopsticks, thinks recreational swimming is a waste of time, can come off as cheap. Has a tendency to believe anything English people say due to their accents. Sometimes lies to people about silly things, like that he once met Buzz Aldrin's brother or that he watches the Food Channel all the time.

Chester's Strengths: Passion for people, quick learner, super nice, good conversationalist, fiscally frugal, and does a spot-on impression of Milton Berle. Has a high metabolism due to eating seven tiny meals a day. Can spot someone's love language within five minutes of knowing them. Has the looks of a regional newscaster. He is a careful voter and actually reads each measure. Unlike Chuck Nary, he is cool and calm. Treats his body as a temple. His only indulgence is a cigar and a pint of absinthe to celebrate a successful kidnapping return.

- - - - - - - - - - - - - - - - - - -

To: Grady Thoms
From: Mair Pearson
Re: Chester Biggles's Character Profile

Grady, creating a new protagonist is not a good idea. You should keep Chuck Nary alive. Give him a chance to sober up and redeem himself.
Mair

- - - - - - - - - - - - - - - - - - -

To: Mair Pearson
Cc: Bill Williams
From: Grady Thoms
Subject: Chester Dies

Mair, Chester Biggles did not last very long in Bolivia. While he was a gentleman, intelligent, and easy to control, I didn't create him to be very tough. After his meeting with Pubano at the bakery, Chester drove downtown to look for a drug mule named Gus. Gus is not a drug mule like you're thinking in human terms, but an actual animal. The drug mule is trained to return to Hector Raul's drug lab after it delivers pouches of cocaine to the runners downtown. Chester planned to sneak on the mule and ride it back to the lab after the delivery.

Chester's mistake was that he did not plan on the mule being trained in ki kee ning, a form of kung fu that involves only kicking. It is specifically designed for donkeys, mules, and men born with no arms. When Chester tries to board Gus (named after my favorite Disney movie), the drug mule kicks him in the stomach. While Chester is doubled over, Gus kicks him in the head and knocks him out. He actually dies from eternal bleeding from the gut shot.

Mair, I know what I'm talking about here because I know a guy who got kicked in the chest by a horse. You should never walk up behind a horse while smoking a cigar. They will try to stomp it out. Ironically, that horse died a week later when it got confused during a lightning storm and ran into a burning barn.

With Chester Biggles dead and Chuck Nary a hopeless drunk, what should I do now? Introduce another character? I feel I no longer have direction or a clear story arc. Maybe I should scrap *Mr. Nary* and start a new book. I could try something easier like writing a children's book. One idea I have is a fun tale about a family of rats during the bubonic plague. It helps children learn about the plague in an educational way and how history can repeat itself if we don't wash our hands.

I have come to the conclusion to burn *Mr. Nary* and start a new project.
Thanks,
Grady

- - - - - - - - - - - - - - - - - - -

To: Grady Thoms
From: Mair Pearson
Re: Chester Dies

Grady, writing a children's book is not as easy as it sounds and does not guarantee success (unless your name is Madonna). Keep working on *Mr. Nary*. Chester Biggles's death might be the best thing that could have happened. I was not feeling him as the protagonist. Find a way to gain control of Chuck Nary and finish the book.
Mair

- - - - - - - - - - - - - - - - - - -

To: Mair Pearson
Cc: Bill Williams
From: Grady Thoms
Subject: Burned My Book

Mair, it is too late, I burned my book. Last night, I invited some friends and family over to Chet's house for a BBQ with the intention of destroying *Mr. Nary* in front of them in a therapeutic ceremony I dubbed "The Dream

Is Over." About twenty unaware guests showed, including my parents, my cousin Jesse, and Jenny.

When people arrived, they were led to the backyard where Chet and I stood in black robes next to a small charcoal grill I had just purchased at Lowe's. My manuscript sat on a small table near a canister of lighter fluid. To make the book appear larger, I double-spaced and reprinted it twice. Most of the guests did not seem too concerned with the plan to burn my book, but some were upset when told there would be no food.

Chet spoke first. He said sometimes you have to let the dreams of the ones you love die. He added that we live in a society that encourages others way too much and often lies, especially to children, about their abilities. He used his niece's paintings and wife's piano playing as examples.

I spoke next, saying I mostly disagreed with what Chet had just said. My feeling is that I have the ability to write a good book but became a classic example of when an author becomes too passionate. The project became too emotional, I said, and it spiraled out of control. *Mr. Nary* was consuming me. The book must be destroyed in a symbolic manner, such as a public burning.

After my words, I put the manuscript into the metal cylinder and soaked it with lighter fluid. I invited anyone else to come up and squirt lighter fluid on it as well, as a sign you support my decision to burn this book. A line quickly formed and nearly everyone participated, except for Jenny and my surly Uncle Craig, who as a Vietnam vet opposes any sort of public demonstration or protest. He called me a book-burning Nazi and said I owed him a bratwurst or something of equal value.

A few minutes later, I lit a match and dropped it on the stack of papers, which caused a huge ball of flame, knocking me back. The wind swiftly carried the glowing papers across the yard, forcing Chet and I to scramble in our bulky robes to step on the flaky embers. It was a scene I wished Jenny had not witnessed.

When the last of the flames were extinguished, a few people clapped, and others approached me with encouragement. It was the first time my dad hugged me since my high school graduation. Chet then wanted to sing *the Doxology,* but I didn't see how that was relevant.

So that's it, 308 reprinted double-spaced pages up in smoke. I'm done

with *Mr. Nary.* Bill and Mair, I am sorry I wasted your time.
Thanks,
Grady

- - - - - - - - - - - - - - - - - - -

To: Grady Thoms
From: Mair Pearson
Re: Burned My Book

Grady, that was intense. I agree with your guests about being upset at being invited to a BBQ with no food. You could have at least provided some potato salad.

Listen, every writer faces discouragement. Please do not let it end here. Every successful writer has been rejected. But the most important thing is that a writer not reject him or herself. I trust *Mr. Nary* is still saved on your computer. Bill says you need to continue to work on the book, and I agree.

Chuck Nary is your hero. Yes, he has his flaws, but I have faith he will stop drinking, control his temper, and pull his life back together.
Mair

- - - - - - - - - - - - - - - - - - -

To: Mair Pearson
Cc: Bill Williams
From: Grady Thoms
Subject: Jenny Ended Our Relationship

Mair, I received a text this morning from Jenny saying "we shud talk." I asked her if she was "*free L8er 2day?*" She said "*she was.*"

Jenny came by later to say she was very disappointed to see me quit on *Mr. Nary.* She said she didn't want to date somebody who would give up on their dream so easily. Can you believe that? She thought we were dating! I thought we were just friends. Apparently the times we were hanging out were actual dates.

Now that I realize she was my girlfriend, I have to find a way to get her back. I don't think I can start working on *Mr. Nary* again, or I'll look like a fool. While it's true the book is still saved on my computer, I've already burned it in a symbolic ceremony in front of family and friends. It was caught on tape. There are thirty-two photos of the event on Chet's Facebook page in an album he titled, "Setting fire to Grady's horrible, horrible mistake."

Even if I decided to finish the book, I doubt I could get back on track. Chuck Nary is a mess, Chester Biggles is dead, and Pubano is incapable. How did things get so complicated? I just wanted to write a book out of inspiration. It hasn't been easy, and I would rather give up.

I told Jenny that I wanted to continue to date her but finishing the book would be nearly impossible now. I lost confidence in my ability to control the story. None of it makes sense to me anymore. My cousin Jesse thinks I should do whatever it takes to keep Jenny. Girls like her come along once in a great while. He said I should not trade her for granite.

Jenny left me with her favorite Elbert Hubbard quote. She said, "God will not look me over for medals, degrees, or diplomas, but for scars." It almost brought tears to my eyes. Almost.

Thanks,

Grady

- - - - - - - - - - - - - - - - - - - -

To: Grady Thoms
From: Mair Pearson
Re: Jenny Ended Our Relationship

Grady, Jenny is right. While it is true the book may fail to be a commercial success, the feeling of accomplishment in itself is a great reward. Remember what Chet said about Michael Jordan and Benjamin Franklin regarding the foreword? All of the greats have failed.

In case you forgot, Bill gave you a deadline of six months to finish *Mr. Nary*. That was over four months ago. Are you going to go back on your original agreement? You have work to do.

I would not worry about your family and friends. You should have a rebirthing ceremony. It happens all the time with Bill's writers. Invite everyone back to Chet's house for a BBQ. Have food this time. You could create a fake

Word document showing your contract with Bill. I will send you our letterhead. Sign it and show it to the group. Say you have no choice but to go on.

We need you to keep writing. It's all smiles in the office when we hear from you.

Mair

- - - - - - - - - - - - - - - - - - - -

To: Mair Pearson
Cc: Bill Williams
From: Grady Thoms
Subject: Book Rebirthing Ceremony

Mair, I forgot about the deadline from Bill. I guess I'm legally bound. On top of that, I have to finish the book if the alternative means losing Jenny, who I just learned was my former girlfriend.

Thank you for the idea of the ceremonial rebirth. As you suggested, I created a contract from Bill using the letterhead. I hope he doesn't mind, but I made the agreement a five-book deal where I own sole possession of any merchandizing and action figures produced from the Chuck Nary™ franchise. I plan to frame this contract and store it in a classy display case.

To give the contract credibility, I will include a letter from Bill's fictitious attorney Alford P. Winslow, who threatens me with litigation if I do not complete the book on time. I want this ceremony to be convincing. Chet printed out a story he found online about a writer who went missing while hiking in Washington. We will tell people he was one of Bill's authors who tried to get out of finishing a book. It's important I show the gravity of the situation to my father, who gave me a twenty-five-dollar gift card to the Olive Garden in support of me giving up writing. I don't want to give it back.

After I show the contents of the glass case, which clearly puts my life in danger, I will read a few selections of *Mr. Nary* while Chet's wife plays the piano. She knows a couple Sweetwater songs, so the evening will be topical. We will then serve tacos during a question-and-answer period.

Later I will tell Jenny that when I set out to do something, I finish it, threats or no threats. It will be painful to go on, I will say, but sometimes a man does crazy things for love. Hopefully, Jenny will be moved. When she smiles and shows her braces with all those rubber bands, my heart melts.

Suddenly, I'm excited to go back to Bolivia.

Thanks,

Grady

- - - - - - - - - - - - - - - - - -

To: Grady Thoms
From: Mair Pearson
Re: Book Rebirthing Ceremony

Grady, this is not exactly what I had in mind, but I should have known. After the ceremony, let's focus solely on the book. There have been too many distractions. My workload has increased, and I do not have the time to approve which topics you should bring up on your next date.
Mair

- - - - - - - - - - - - - - - - - -

To: Mair Pearson
Cc: Bill Williams
From: Grady Thoms
Subject: Chuck Nary Still Drinking

Mair, I was hoping that after taking some time off I would find Chuck Nary in a better place. Unfortunately, he is still drunk and living on the streets. He has even begun to have serious discussions with imaginary people. I thought it might help if I wrote a couple lines about Nary finding an old picture of his mother in his wallet. Perhaps seeing her would give him the courage to stop boozing. Yet all it did was cause him to purchase two bottles of malt liquor and a pack of Virginia menthol cigarettes, the kind his mother smokes.

It has been difficult to try to help Chuck Nary. My cousin Jesse says sometimes we can't fix the ones we love, no matter what we do or say. Some people are put in our lives just to be loved. That's true for Chuck Nary. I will continue to write and let the story unfold, but I must warn you, it may not have a happy ending.

On the other side of town, Pubano is becoming desperate. The new detective he hired was kicked to death by a drug mule. Time is running short for him to find Mr. Nary. Sophia's paid assassins are getting close. There have been reports of an obnoxious gringo in bullfighter pants badgering shop owners for free samples in El Centro. A fight is coming on.

Thanks,

Grady

May

To: Mair Pearson
Cc: Bill Williams
From: Grady Thoms
Subject: Items for Sale

Mair, the camping gear business is tanking due to the economy. Plus, people are starting to realize camping is a lot of work and not that much fun. I need some supplementary income.

I will be selling a few of my personal belongings so I can continue to work on *Mr. Nary.* Let me know if you, Bill, or anyone at the office is interested in the following items:

Bob Dole for President Bumper Sticker—I have seven left. $1 each

A Painting of My Grandfather—This original painting is of my grandfather in a wheelchair being pushed through a cemetery in late fall by Andy Griffith (Grandpa was a big fan of *Matlock*). It is foreboding, ironic, darkly funny, nonsensical, and all that other crap people look for in works of art. $75

VHS Sequel Collection Tapes—For several years, I collected sequels to great movies. I have *Robocop* 2, *Young Guns* 2, *Gremlins* 2 (taped from TV, missing first five minutes), *Caddyshack II*, *City Slickers* 2: *The Legend of Curly's Gold*, *Teen Wolf Too* (broken, must rewind manually with fingers). $2 each

6 Metal Coat Hangers—If you don't need them for yourself, coat hangers are a perfect complementary gift item to give along with a sweater or a shirt. A lot of people give shirts without thinking about the hanger. They are also good for roasting marshmallows. $0.50 each

Personalized Food Dish for Pet—Do you have a dog or cat named Scooter? If so, it's your lucky day. I have a food dish with the name "Scooter" on it. If you don't, you might want to consider buying the food bowl and changing your pet's name to Scooter. $15

The Stone that may or may not have slain Goliath—When my cousin Jesse visited the Middle East several years ago, he went hiking southwest of Jerusalem, near the Valley of Elah (the spot where David killed the giant). While he was walking, he found a smooth stone lying in a creek bed and noticed it would be perfect for a sling. He decided to bring it back to the States. Having heard about this potential monumental discovery, I traded him my Vlade Divac rookie card for the stone. Given the possible significance of the artifact, I cannot accept less than $300 for it. If you decide to purchase the stone, you will also receive: a glass case, a copy of Jesse Thoms' travel itinerary with receipts proving he was in Israel, and a genuine certificate signed by both Jesse and I stating "This stone may or may not be the one that killed Goliath."

Thanks,
Grady

- - - - - - - - - - - - - - - - - - -

To: Grady Thoms
From: Mair Pearson
Re: Items for Sale

Grady, what is going on with your book? Has Pubano found Chuck Nary?
Mair

- - - - - - - - - - - - - - - - - - -

To: Mair Pearson
Cc: Bill Williams
From: Grady Thoms
Subject: The Two Assassins

Mair, the two assassins Sophia hired have located Chuck Nary. They are monitoring his movements and will wait for the opportune time to take him out, most likely at night. Luckily for Nary, they have yet to learn of his ongoing inebriated state of mind.

One of the assassins, Clyde, is a French-Canadian experienced in explosives. Clyde used to be a bus driver in Quebec but got into assassintry after getting fired for driving while reading the children steamy French romance novels over the bus intercom.

How do you suppose one becomes an assassin? You can't go to school for it, I've looked. It's probably a trade you're born into, such as politics or the family pawnshop. I wonder if assassins are embarrassed to talk about what they do, like high school art teachers, who had something better in mind for their lives but had to settle.

The other assassin, Razon, is a young Hispanic man from Los Angeles. Being new to the assassin world, he came along to learn from Clyde. Razon and Clyde are not the best at what they do. In fact, they are very average. Again, this is to add to the uniqueness of my novel. How come when you watch movies or read thrillers, everyone is always "highly trained" or "the top in their field"? They can't all be the best. Some have to be mediocre assassins, barely eking their way from kill to kill.

Sophia hires Razon and Clyde because they are cheap. Mr. Nary killed three of her other assassins, and she is running low on money. Sophia is not optimistic. Clyde's reputation is not great. He is known as a coward who sometimes kills the wrong person. Clyde successfully completes only about a third of his assignments. A good assassin should kill around 85 percent of his targets.

Thanks,

Grady

- - - - - - - - - - - - - - - - - - -

To: Mair Pearson
Cc: Bill Williams
From: Grady Thoms
Subject: Assassin Research Using Paintball

Mair, Chet thought it would be a good idea to go paintballing last weekend in order to get into the mindset of an assassin. We dug up our old ski goggles, borrowed a couple of camouflaged tank tops from my dad, and headed out to *Swell Times Paintball* in Gresham. To cover the cost, we stopped at a clinic to sell some of my plasma. Chet refuses to sell his plasma or donate blood. He's afraid the person who receives his blood might later commit a heinous crime and leave his DNA at the scene.

Chet thought we should invite Jenny to come along. He says assassins sometimes have to shoot the ones they love. If I really want to dive into their world, I will have to know what it feels like to have my current flame in the scope of my rifle and pull the trigger. Jenny thought it sounded fun. Since my resuming my book, she has agreed to hang out with me again. She used the words "hang out," so I don't know if we are dating or not. I will look for clues.

At the paintball center, a pudgy man with greasy black hair rented us the only paint guns we could afford—single shooters with a propensity to malfunction. The paint balls had to be manually loaded into the shooting chamber and cocked back using a series of levers and pulleys after each shot. Muskets from the American Revolution could shoot faster. I noticed others entering the building with their own semiautomatics with the capability of firing five rounds per second. Apparently, there are entire catalogs dedicated to this sport.

The pudgy man, Ronald, told us that we should wear something more than tank tops. He said the paint balls can leave contusions, bruises, and even break the skin. Chet assured him we wanted to be nimble during battle. Long sleeves would just slow us down. He asked us if we wanted to wear cups, but we declined. Again, we wanted to be nimble.

A professional paintball team known as Extreme Velocity was waiting around for a challenge. The four men, dressed in army fatigues with masks and holding weapons ready for biological warfare, were looking for a friendly match to tune up their skills. In a couple weeks, they will be participating in the Run Kill Die Open in Boise. It's a tournament sponsored by Red Bull so you know it's legit.

The leader of Extreme Velocity, code name Vice Grip, said he didn't want to shoot a girl, so Jenny would have to play with them. She was handed a new gun and full gear sponsored by Raymond's Semiautomatic Hunting Supplies. Chet and I found a grizzled, wiry man standing nearby who we thought could join our team, which we dubbed Gorilla Warfare. We figured he was probably going to be good because he had sewn army patches on his jacket and wore a purple beret. Earl introduced himself and claimed to be recruited by the CIA, FBI, and KGB. He turned down that life so he could be closer to his granddaughter, who he is not allowed to see. He started to give Chet and me orders on what to do right away.

A few minutes later, a heavy set of identical twins reluctantly entered the building. Leonard and Bruce, tall oafs who shared the same blank stare, poor posture, and Winterhawks jerseys, lumbered to the counter to rent their guns. They were not happy to be there.

As it turns out, it was the twins' birthday, and their mother forced them to paintball. Every year, she makes the reclusive brothers try a new experience. Last year they went deep-sea fishing. The year before, they went spelunking in Nevada. Next year, they might go wine tasting. Leonard and Bruce would join Gorilla Warfare. The teams were set.

The game was Capture the Flag. Earl gathered us around at our end of the arena and talked about the chain of command. As head general, Earl would creep up the left side quietly while Chet and I, the foot soldiers, would flank up the right to occupy Extreme Velocity. Leonard and Bruce, who Earl referred to as expendable militiamen, would guard the flag. Unfortunately, the twins would be necessary casualties of war, he said. Earl said a quick prayer and gave the official the thumbs-up. The whistle blew.

We were immediately under attack. I followed Chet to the right with my head down under a hail of gunfire. Somehow they were already in shooting range. Chet dove behind a stack of rubber foam logs, and I followed. Pellets whizzed over our heads with regularity. I tried to peek around the side, but bark chips flung up in my face from the rain of bullets. It was like the beginning of *Saving Private Ryan*.

Chet reached over the top of the logs to fire a warning shot. His weapon jammed and then his index finger was struck with a paint ball, which didn't break. He howled and flung his gun down to grab his hand. Now curled up in the fetal position, Chet began yelling for a medic, but in vain. I noticed his bare shoulder was discolored from the result of another shot. Again, the pellet did not break. For you to be called out of the game, the paint ball has to burst open. Technically speaking, Chet was still in the game.

I glanced back to see how the twins were doing defending the flag. Behind a bale of hay in the corner, one of the brothers lay flat on his stomach, his hands raised in surrender. The other brother had left the arena to sit in the stands, where he was eating an Abba-Zaba and playing with his iPhone. Earl was nowhere to be seen.

It turns out that Earl had been dead for a while. As soon as the whistle blew, he attempted to seek refuge behind a large rubber tire. Earl was shot three times before he could reach it, and the third pellet finally broke on his neck. He played a total of eight seconds. Earl claimed how Extreme Velocity was smart in taking out the leader of Gorilla Warfare. Cut off the head of the dragon and the beast will surely fall, he said. I've never met anyone so delusional as Earl.

Extreme Velocity realized we were no match and decided to split up the teams. We played a few more games which were more competitive. I never got the chance to shoot Jenny, but I doubt I would have if given the chance. I guess I wouldn't make a very good assassin. This experience may not help me with understanding the mind of a hired killer, but now I can write about the tendencies of identical twins in combative situations.

Thanks,

Grady

- - - - - - - - - - - - - - - - - - -

To: Grady Thoms
From: Mair Pearson
Re: Assassin Research Using Paintball

Grady, I saw the length of this e-mail and chose not to read it. These are the kind of distractions I was talking about. I do not have time to read lengthy e-mails relating to your odd escapades which may or may not have to do with the book.

I forwarded this on to Ed Simmons in accounting, who thoroughly enjoys your exploits, and he said it is well worth the read. Maybe I will come back to it when I do not have three manuscripts sitting on my desk in need of attention.

Mair

To: Bill Williams
Cc: Mair Pearson
From: Grady Thoms
Subject: Tax Write-offs

Bill, my extension is up, and it's time to get taxes done. I'm wondering what sort of purchases authors can write off as work expenses? So far I have receipts from Swell Times Paintball, Murphy's Irish Pub, and the Portland Zoo, where I observed the behaviors of monkeys and petted some goats and llamas for about an hour (for research).

What else can I list as expenses? I've been using my apartment to work on *Mr. Nary*, as well as hosting BRAG meetings, so it looks like I can write off my rent. Chet thinks I can claim just about anything remotely related to *Mr. Nary* as a work expense since I'm counting on this book for the majority of my future income. It would be in the best interest of the IRS if they cut me a break now so later I can make this country some decent money.

Thanks,

Grady

- - - - - - - - - - - - - - - - - - -

To: Grady Thoms
Cc: Mair Pearson
From: Bill Williams
Re: Tax Write-offs

Grady, in addition to writing about hired assassins and twins in combative situations, you will soon be able to write knowingly about tax audits. I expect you will be receiving one. Trust me, the IRS will not wait for you to make money. Like a strapped bookie, they want their money now.

Furthermore, you cannot write off food, alcohol, or entertainment unless you can prove it was absolutely necessary in writing the book. Claiming your rent or even part of your rent as tax deductible is also a surefire way to receive an audit. Consult a tax adviser.

Regards,

Bill

To: Bill Williams
Cc: Mair Pearson
From: Grady Thoms
Re: Tax Write-offs

Bill, I met with Chet's taxpayer, Charles Loots, who says I can write off almost anything I want. According to him, I'm small fish to the IRS. Charles (who prefers to be called "Loophole") claims they don't even look at tax returns of anyone making under thirty thousand dollars. He says if I include photocopies of some random receipts and sign the return with my left hand, I should be fine. I think I can trust him. He was wearing a suit he personally had tailored in Chinatown with a Jerry Garcia tie he got from Nordstrom Rack, where Nordstrom sends their best stuff.

Loophole is a pretty cool guy. I could spend all day in his office. He has a minifridge stocked with Dr. Pepper and Mr. Pibb. He has one of those kickback putting cups. He even has a framed Magic Eye 3-D poster signed by David Blaine. Loophole pretty much has it all figured out. The man works only thirty hours a week and vacations in Reno three times a year. He owns a pair of golf sandals and has his steak shipped to *him*. I could go on and on about Loophole. You guys should totally hire him.

Sorry to bother you with my taxes. I'll try keep my inquiries to literary topics from now on.

Thanks,

Grady

- - - - - - - - - - - - - - - - - -

To: Grady Thoms
Cc: Mair Pearson
From: Bill Williams
Re: Tax Write-offs

Grady, thank you for telling us about the Charles "Loophole" Loots, but I think we would have better luck sticking with the fictitious attorney you assigned us during your rebirthing ceremony. Even though he does not exist, I would feel more comfortable with Alford P. Winslow handling our affairs.

Regards,

Bill

- - - - - - - - - - - - - - - - - - -

To: Mair Pearson
Cc: Bill Williams
From: Grady Thoms
Subject: Chapter Titles

Mair, I know I haven't had titles for the chapters, but I'm going to have one for chapter 17. It will be called *Chapter 17: The Most Intense Chapter Yet.* My readers need to be warned before they begin reading. It's like when your parents tell you to sit down before giving you the news they are separating and will no longer be paying for your car insurance. The title basically tells you to sit down and get ready for a heavy dose of drama.

I thought about going back and naming all the chapters. What do you think? Bill's book doesn't have chapter titles, and so initially I didn't want titles either. Now I might be leaning toward having them. Here is what I would call the first seventeen chapters if I change my mind:

Chapter 1: The Call
Chapter 2: Nary Answers
Chapter 3: Bullfighter Pants
Chapter 4: Hot on the Trail
Chapter 5: Trail Goes Cold
Chapter 6: Trail Heating Up Again
Chapter 7: Little Orphan, Why So Quiet?
Chapter 8: Dead End, Gringo
Chapter 9: Landlocked Situations
Chapter 10: Epic Car Chase
Chapter 12: Pey Dies . . . or Does He?
Chapter 13: Pey Does Die
Chapter 14: Looking through an Empty Bottle

I will send over chapter 17 later tonight.
Thanks,
Grady

- - - - - - - - - - - - - - - - - - -

To: Grady Thoms
From: Mair Pearson
Re: Chapter Titles

Grady, Bill is for any changes in which *Mr. Nary* will distinguish itself from *The Missionary*. I happen to like the chapter titles, as do others here in the office.
Mair

- - - - - - - - - - - - - - - - - - -

To: Mair Pearson
Cc: Bill Williams
From: Grady Thoms
Subject: Chapter 17: The Most Intense Chapter Yet

Mair, here is chapter 17. It starts with Chuck Nary in bad shape on the mean streets of La Paz. The bumbling assassins are closing in. The fight will be even.

CHAPTER 17: THE MOST INTENSE CHAPTER YET

The shadows of the tall buildings in El Centro grew long and square-shaped. Street merchants promptly closed up their carts and pushed on, giving way to drug dealers, palm readers, and demon-possessed magicians. Some of the magicians were quite good actually, and earned a decent reputation among American college travelers. The palm readers were avoided however, mostly because they told tourists they might get mugged later, which often turned prophetic but is not something you should say as an entertainer.

Chuck Nary sat against a tree in the Plaza Park, an empty bottle of chardonnay laying at his feet. His bullfighter pants, tattered and dirty, reminded him of Pey. He blamed himself. It should have been me who was shot, thought Nary. I would give up my subscription to Gals 'n' Guns for Pey to still be alive. He was in the bargaining phase of grief. Lifting himself onto his feet, he rubbed his eyes and pointed his feet toward the mercado across the street. He needed another drink.

* * *

Down the park and hidden in some brush, a pair of binoculars kept track of Chuck Nary's movements. The French Canadian kept meticulous notes. Clyde jotted down that Nary looked a little like his Uncle Pierre, a towering man who showed up every Christmas with a different woman. Sometimes these girlfriends would have a child his age he could play with. Those were the best Christmases.

His young counterpart, Razon, sat in the shade nearby, looking bored. Clyde was starting to dislike him. Every so often, Razon would make comments on how he thought being an assassin would involve more killing and less walking around looking for croissants. Earlier in the day, they had gotten into a heated argument when Razon asked how someone could be French AND Canadian. Clyde exploded in anger. It is not a topic you bring up with FCs.

Clyde took comfort knowing he would not have to spend much more time with Razon. Darkness was settling in, and soon the American would be taken out. The plan was to have Razon approach Mr. Nary as a poor kid asking for money. At that point, Clyde would attack Razon, pretending to mug him. Certainly Nary would intervene and tackle Clyde. While they were engaged, Razon would come up from behind and shoot Mr. Nary in the head. After two days of planning, this was the best idea they had.

* * *

Chuck Nary sat back down under a familiar tree, two small bottles of Rose Zinfandel pokeing out of his pocket. He was in the mood for something light and summery, with a crisp finish. Unaware that two assassins were closing in, Nary twisted the cap from one of the bottles and began to gulp down the sweet nectar.

Nary wondered what Pubano would think of his drunk and filthy friend now. Little did he know that Pubano was in dire need of his help. Alegria was being held hostage in a basement room with no mirrors, driving the vain woman slowly mad. She was starting to forget what she looked like. A few more days and she would lose all interest in her appearance forever.

With the sunlight nearly gone, a beggar shuffled by Nary, his hand outstretched. Mr. Nary ignored it. He had been fooled into giving money to the homeless before. Once he gave a couple dollars to a transient in Houston desperately needing $1.80 for a bus ticket back to his home in Galveston. A few days later, the same man was again short $1.80. Nary agreed to help but advised him to stop coming downtown without the proper change.

At that moment, a thin figure in a black cap lurched out of the darkness and grabbed the beggar by the shoulders. Speaking in a heavy French accent with subtle notes of Canadian, the man claimed to have an epee under his jacket and would use it if the beggar did not give him money.

"Gihf me oll zee monee you hohve, ehh. I fhant to puht et en mah pockhat!" Clyde reached into his coat in a threatening matter.

The young beggar pleaded with the robber, saying he had two small children in wheelchairs at home. The aggressor scoffed and told him nothing could stop him from taking his money for medicine to heal the children's legs. The conversation was in earshot of Chuck Nary, yet he made no move. He was settling into a nice white wine buzz, the kind you get when you're hosting a yacht party and everything is going swimmingly. The last thing he wanted was a fight.

Unfortunately for Clyde and Razon, two robed bishops shuffling by overheard the confrontation. The men, on their way to evening mass at Saint Edmundo, wasted no time to intervene. One of the bishops, a balding man of natural stoutness, shouted "Algo!" as he grabbed the French Canadian from behind. The other bishop, taller and just as feisty, began throwing open-hand punches at the assailant's head.

Chuck Nary watched the scene unfold with mild amusement. He could tell the fearless bishops had been in a brawl or two. The mugger crouched down to protect himself from the onslaught. He yelled at the beggar to do something, as if the man he was trying to rob would come to his rescue. In slow motion, the beggar reached inside his coat and pulled out a Beretta revolver with an attached suppressor. He calmly walked up to the wrestling men and fired six rounds. All three men slumped over dead.

Nary immediately bolted up, his mind in overdrive. A beggar with a silencer, this was a hit man. He wheeled around the tree looking for his next cover. How could he be so stupid, exposing himself in the open like this? Feeling stiff, Nary ambled toward the mercado. His bullfighter pants looked good on him, but they were not conducive for running.

* * *

Razon leaned down to check the pulse of Clyde. He was gone. The young assassin did not plan to kill his partner until finishing the job, but the opportunity presented itself. Now he could collect the whole payment, not just the measly 25 percent unfairly promised to him. He simply needed to complete the assignment. Razon pivoted toward the tree where Chuck Nary had been propped. The American had slipped away into the darkness.

Walking at a brisk pace, Razon thought about where Nary would hide. In the last two days, the only place he had been outside the park was the market down the street. Surely he would go somewhere with familiar surroundings. Tucking his gun back into his coat, Razon trotted toward the lights at the other side of the plaza.

* * *

Inside the market, Chuck Nary staggered up to the burly cashier perched on a stool behind the counter and held up his hand to his ear to show the international sign for telephone.

"Policia! Policia! Nueve-Uno-Uno!" his unused voice rasped. Unknown to Chuck Nary, the emergency number in Bolivia is 1-1-0, not 9-1-1. The owner ignored the crazy gringo and continued to count money, keeping his eyes below his bowler hat. It was near closing time.

Nary backpedaled to the far wall of the cramped market, inhaling quick breaths. There was a small office with a toilet and mop in the corner but no exit. He dropped on all fours and crawled behind a pallet of burlap sacks filled with beans, frantically scanning the sparse shelves for something to defend himself.

From the front of the market, Nary heard the owner mumble to a patron who had just entered. Pfft. Pfft. The sound of the silencer cut through the cold, dry air. The man's round body flopped to the floor, knocking over his stool. Now he would never know the joys of holding a grandchild or even the joys of holding a regular child, as he was not married.

Nary knew he had just seconds to act. Staying low, he peeked around the burlap sacks. Down the aisle, the killer's shape reflected off the glossy body of a charango, a stringed instrument Nary recognized from his Wikipedia research on Bolivia.

The figure approached slowly. With each step, Nary could feel the planks of the battered wooden floor squeezing together. The assassin was a few paces away. He paused. Something on one of the shelves caught his attention. Gradually poking his eyes above the line of sight, Nary could see the killer looking at souvenir shot glasses. He had singled out two of the glasses, deciding which to take. One featured an Andean condor. The other branded an outline of the country with a red star symbolizing the capitol of La Paz. He would take just one out of principle.

Mr. Nary seized the moment to dart behind a barrel of dried peppers to the adjacent aisle. The entrance was roughly two-thirds of a bowling lane away. He could make a mad dash for it but hesitated, as the door was now closed. Nary couldn't remember if it required a push or pull from the inside. One wrong push when a pull was needed would mean certain death. To make matters worse, there was no reminder on the handle. Damn these Second-World countries without signs directing a proper way to exit, thought Nary. Even with a flawless door opening, the assassin would have time to fire one, maybe two clear shots. How good of an aim was he? He hadn't missed so far.

Out of the corner of his eye, Nary noticed a pair of rusty sheep shears leaning against a crate of archery equipment. He would have to somehow use those shears as a weapon. His best defense would be to bum-rush the man while brandishing the shears in a threatening manner. The shears combined with the element of surprise might give him a chance. With great care, Nary reached for the shears while thinking the term "bum-rush" was probably an unfair expression toward bums. He took a deep breath and prepared for a suicidal charge.

With a quick burst, Nary scrambled out from behind the barrel and lunged toward his enemy. The young killer, now facing in Nary's direction, stiffened upright and briefly froze, his face stuck in horrified puzzlement.

Mr. Nary was near striking distance when the assassin finally woke, raising his weapon to fire. Nary stumbled, his mind alert but body still drunk, toward the feet of the young killer. Using all his force, Nary sunk the tip of the shears into the right boot of the assailant. Blood exploded up the blade and onto Nary's face. A piercing cry shook the air. The assassin crumpled to the floor, convulsing in agony next to his broken Andean condor shot glass. Leaping onto his feet, Nary picked up the revolver and stood over the hired goon, holding the muzzle six inches from his head.

"Who sent you? Was it that woman, Sophia? She must be getting pretty desperate to send a chump like you."

The young assassin wailed while holding the handle of the shears stuck in his foot. Intense pain shot through his spine. He shouted at his misfortune.

"Nooo! Nooo!"

Pfft. Chuck Nary ended his misery. He might have let him go if he thought the poor bastard would not have died from blood loss. The kid couldn't have been more than twenty. It was a shame.

On the way out of the market, Nary grabbed two more bottles of chardonnay and glanced over to the register where the owner had been counting his money. His body now lay in a heap on the floor behind the counter. On the wall above, a small spatter of blood glistened on a painting of the Virgin Mary.

"Looks like business is dead." Nary straightened his posture. He would do his drinking in a new part of town.

Mair, do you think this is too gory? You should have seen what I originally wrote. At first, I had Nary stabbing Razon in the eyes with shears but thought better of it. There might be people with heart conditions reading this novel. I don't want to cause a controversy like those guys who made the *Face of Death* movies.

Thanks,
Grady

- - - - - - - - - - - - - - - - - - -

To: Mair Pearson
Cc: Bill Williams
From: Grady Thoms
Subject: CAPS LOCK BROKEN

MAIR, SOMETHING IS WRONG WITH MY COMPUTER. I CAN'T GET THE CAPS LOCK BUTTON TO TURN OFF. IT SEEMS LIKE I'M YELLING BUT I'M NOT. I'M CALM. PLEASE DON'T FEEL AS IF I'M ANGRY WITH YOU. THIS IS MY NORMAL TYPING VOICE.

ANYWAY, DID YOU AND BILL GET A CHANCE TO READ CHAPTER 17 YET? NO BIG DEAL IF YOU HAVEN'T YET. AGAIN, I'M NOT ANGRY. IT MIGHT SEEM LIKE I'M UPSET BECAUSE OF THE ALL CAPS BUT I'M NOT. THE COMPUTER IS BROKEN. I WISH YOU COULD SEE ME. I'M CALM BUT THIS E-MAIL IS NOT CONVEYING THAT.

SORRY,
GRADY

To: Grady Thoms
From: Mair Pearson
Re: CAPS LOCK BROKEN

Grady, I can tell you are not yelling but thank you for the warning. I do hope you get it fixed as this reminds me of my mother's e-mails when she writes "FOUND A GREAT APPLE PIE RECIPE!!" or "SAW THE MAYOR AT SAFEWAY!" Or my personal favorite, "BABY GAP IS HAVING A SALE, WHEN ARE YOU GOING TO HAVE BABIES?! ;)." (She follows up her e-mails with a winky-smiley face as if this makes it okay to say anything she wants.)

   We have not read chapter 17. I will get to it sometime this week.
Mair

- - - - - - - - - - - - - - - - - - -

To: Mair Pearson
From: Grady Thoms
Re: CAPS LOCK BROKEN

Mair, I fixed it. The caps button was stuck because of a popcorn kernel. Not sure how it got there, I don't even eat popcorn. See, I told you I was not yelling. It just looked like I was.

   You better hurry up and read chapter 17. I'm almost done with chapter 18. Pubano and Chuck Nary reunite!
Thanks,
Grady

- - - - - - - - - - - - - - - - - - -

To: Grady Thoms
From: Mair Pearson
Re: CAPS LOCK BROKEN

Chapter 17 was everything we have come to expect from you. There is a lot of work to be done in the showing vs telling department, but you can worry about that in the rewrites. Keep going!
Mair

To: Mair Pearson
Cc: Bill Williams
From: Grady Thoms
Subject: Touching Scene

Mair, I know my book should be anchored in masculinity, but I just wrote a few paragraphs which will make grown men cry. In chapter 18, there is a sweet reunion between Pubano and Chuck Nary. It will make you feel as if you just watched Oprah give away college degrees to stay-at-home moms who never had a chance. Have the tissues ready.

Chuck Nary remained slumped up against a brick wall in a grimy alley which smelled of hobos and fish. Underneath him, a mixture of tears and spilled chardonnay began to form a puddle, taking the shape of what looked like a landlocked country. Perhaps it was this one. His head sank below his heavy heart.

Nary didn't hear the footsteps approach. A stout figure hovered over him. An unmistakable odor, Alpine Brut, wafted above his head. It was Pubano.

"Amigo, I finally fine you!"

"Get away Pubano, I'm a nothing."

"No, I need jhou." The stalky native got behind his friend and strained to pull him up. Nary polished what was left of his wine as Pubano hoisted him onto his feet.

"Senoor, we haff unfinish work leff. My wife, Alegria, they take her. Hector Raul say es either you or her who will die."

"Then it shall be me, Pubano…unless…you're tired of your wife?"

"No, I loff her."

"Yeah well, it should be me then."

Pubano apologetically put his hand on Chuck Nary's shoulder. The chances of retrieving Alegria and keeping Mr. Nary alive were nearly impossible. Tears welled in Pubano's eyes. Nary took a deep breath.

"Could be the end of the road for me, Pubano." Nary shrugged. He had run out of answers and gave in to his vulnerability and weak-

ness. There was nothing left to hide behind. Pubano leaned in.

"In my country, we haff a saying: if you climb a steep mouhtain with a stranger, you will come back down as freins." The portly Bolivian sniffled. "But I haff climb twhenty mouhtains with you, my frein. You are family."

Nary grabbed Pubano and pulled him into his chest, embracing him platonically. Pubano tried to fight back emotion.

But emotion won.

Mair, I didn't know I had this sort of writing in me. Jenny says I keep surprising her with my versatility.
Thanks,
Grady

- - - - - - - - - - - - - - - - - - - -

To: Grady Thoms
From: Mair Pearson
Re: Touching Scene

Grady, I think it was wise to show the weight of the relationship between Pubano and Chuck Nary. Personally, this has been one of my favorite submissions of yours. You have captured the essence of male bonding without stepping over the line.
Mair

- - - - - - - - - - - - - - - - - - - -

To: Mair Pearson
From: Grady Thoms
Re: Touching Scene

Thanks Mair, would you like to endorse my book? I'm looking for authors, publishers, and others in the business to contribute a line or two in support of *Mr. Nary.*
Thanks,
Grady

To: Grady Thoms
From: Mair Pearson
Re: Touching Scene

Grady, I'll have to get back to you on that. If I were to endorse your book, I would write something to the effect of, "*Mr. Nary,* an accidental satire, definitely has a lot of words with characters who may not be as interesting as the author. Despite inconsistencies in the narrative and huge plot holes, it may find a small, cultlike audience who appreciate unintentional parodies." Mair

- - - - - - - - - - - - - - - - - - - -

To: Mair Pearson
Cc: Bill Williams
From: Grady Thoms
Subject: Endorsements

Bill and Mair, as you both know, all thrillers have endorsements from critics and other writers. Besides the two of you, who else can I count on for endorsements? Bill, can you get ahold of Dan Brown or Stephen King? Tell them they will surely want to attach their name to Mr. Nary. They don't even have to write the endorsement, I could do it for them. Also, can I use quotes from Chet and Jesse to promote the book? Here is how I picture the endorsements to look on the back cover:

" …a taut thriller…"
—Bill Williams, coauthor of *The Missionary*

"I couldn't put it down, it was so very taut…"
—David Swanson, coauthor of *The Missionary*

" …exceeds acceptability and is of the upmost coherence."
—Chet Jensen, author's friend

"Mr. Nary is as taut as they come…"
—Dan Brown, *The Vinci Code*

"Other books should strive to be like this taut book."
—Stephen King, writes a lot of books

" . . . definitely…interesting, huge…audience…expected."
—Mair Pearson, works for Bill

"I have to say, it is very good. I would not be surprised if others described it as taut."
—Grady Thoms, author of *Mr. Nary*

"Taut with a capital T."
—Cormac McCarthy, wrote the screenplays for *No Country for Old Men* and *The Road*

"Someone should have warned me how taut this book was . . ."
—Jesse Thoms, author's cousin

Thanks,
Grady

- - - - - - - - - - - - - - - - - - -

To: Grady Thom
Cc: Bill Williams
From: Mair Pearson
Re: Endorsements

Grady, expect some backlash for writing endorsements for the other authors. Generally, people in this industry prefer to write their own reviews and mostly save them for novels they genuinely enjoyed reading.

You certainly did a decent job of chopping up my quote. I can see why film critics take exception when their reviews are taken out of context. Moreover, I do believe it is a bold move to write an endorsement for yourself, but at least you have one honest quote out of the lot.

I noticed you used the word "taut" several times in these fake reviews and not always correctly. Do you know what it means?
Mair

To: Mair Pearson
Cc: Bill Williams
From: Grady Thoms
Subject: Grady Thoms Calendar

Mair, *taut* means well-written, fast-paced, nonstop action. It's a common word used in our industry.

So as part of my grassroots marketing campaign, I am putting together a Grady Thoms calendar. Jesse will take pictures of me in various poses to convey a successful author persona. I plan to give out the first one hundred calendars with a purchase of *Mr. Nary.* The rest we will leave at community bulletin boards, bus stops, and twenty-four-hour fitness locker rooms. Here are the pictures for each month.

January—Grady enjoys his pipe while reading *War and Peace* in a robe next to a brick fireplace.

February—Grady, in his favorite black turtleneck, sips wine while working on an elaborate puzzle.

March—Grady sits at the beach wearing a Yale sweatshirt and reads a complicated book about science.

April—Grady, in an argyle sweater, rides a horse through a vineyard.

May—Grady in a tuxedo plays a tune on the piano while a lovely lady in a fur coat lingers.

June—Grady does community work by wiping oil off of a white swan while wearing a Harvard sweater.

July—Draped in the American flag, Grady crosses the finish line of the Wilsonville Doernbeckers 2k fun run.

August—Grady sports a goatee, black-rimmed glasses, and looks directly at the camera in this classy black-and-white photo.

September—Grady plays pool in the study with a couple of older, distinguished gentlemen while empty bottles of twenty-five-year-old scotch lay about.

October—Using a collage of pictures, Grady plays guitar, wears a graduation gown, and shakes hands with the mayor.

November—Grady and his favorite author, Bill Williams, sit in Bill's study while sharing a cup of cider and a laugh. (Bill, we'll have to plan a time when we can do this.)

December—Grady hands out toys to poor children in a Santa hat as part of the Authors-4-Orphans Foundation, which I might start later.

Thanks,
Grady

- - - - - - - - - - - - - - - - - - - -

To: Grady Thoms
From: Mair Pearson
Re: Grady Thoms Calendar

Grady, please send a few of these calendars to the office. A couple of my coworkers have even offered to pay good money for this "collector item."

Mair

June

To: Mair Pearson
Cc: Bill Williams
From: Grady Thoms
Subject: THE Battle

Mair, chapters 19 and 20 are all about the rescue of Alegria. Chuck Nary is approaching the situation ready to give his life for her release, but he won't go down without a fight. Now that Nary is cleaned up and relatively sober, he and Pubano begin planning the assault on Hector Raul's mansion.

This is where you might be sarcastically thinking, "Oh great, another race against time to save a kidnap victim before she gets cut up to pieces and fed to Doberment Pinchers. Real original." Just wait, this rescue will avoid the clichés.

For starters, the guards at Hector Raul's mansion will not be your typical gun-toting numbskull you see at his drug labs or his illegal penguin breeding compound. No, his personal guards will be attractive women, trained in the arts of poison dart making/blowing. Can you imagine an army of hot South American women (mostly from Brazil) running around blowing poisoned darts? Bill, I think I have your attention now.

On top of that, Hector Raul will not have regular guard dogs. He'll own a trove of spider monkeys that are not well-trained but are very aggressive. They are imprisoned in various tree houses on the compound and forced to watch Steven Seagal movies twenty-four hours a day, making them prone to bite. They are released only in emergencies.

Since the Bolivian navy doesn't have much to do, Pubano has enlisted their help in the rescue attempt of Alegria. Notice how I said "rescue attempt." I haven't decided if they will be successful or not. She might die a horrible death.

Nary and Pubano decide to surprise Hector Raul in broad daylight on a Saturday afternoon, when most of the hot guards are at the open market shopping for sarongs, coconut bras, and materials for dart making. Using the river along his property as an entry point, they will use Piranha Assault boats to motor close to Hector Raul's 6-bedroom, 2.5-bath mansion. Nary, Pubano, and a couple other men (who will probably die) will be dropped off a half-mile up the river. The rest of the infantry will power down below the residence to begin the assault from the south. They will mostly serve as decoys (like Chet and I when we went paintballing).

Pubano was able to obtain some intel on Hector Raul and learned of his troop of unstable spider monkeys. Nary comes up with the idea to bring a sack of fermented Naga Viper peppers, the hottest peppers in the world. He hopes the peppers will burn the monkey's mouths and scatter them back down to the jungles in the lowlands.

Unfortunately for Chuck Nary, Hector Raul has spent years building the monkeys' tolerance to Naga Viper peppers. The peppers only make them mad. Thanks,
Grady

- - - - - - - - - - - - - - - - - - -

To: Grady Thoms
From: Mair Pearson
Re: THE Battle

Grady, I can honestly say your novel has done a decent job of avoiding a lot of clichés (except for the damsel in distress). I can only think of a handful of manuscripts which have used spider monkeys and coconut bra-wearing Brazilians as guards. Good work.
Mair

- - - - - - - - - - - - - - - - - - -

To: Mair Pearson
Cc: Bill Williams
From: Grady Thoms
Subject: Animal Cruelty in Fiction

Mair, as I describe the fight scene in chapter 19, I realize more animals are going to die. So far, this novel has two dead llamas (from the epic car chase), a disabled pigeon, and the death of one annoying capuchin monkey, which Chuck Nary kills for food. Now it looks as if a few of Hector Raul's spider monkeys will die in the battle. It has me thinking, do you think I will hear from animal rights activists?

Chet says it's okay if I kill a few monkeys in the battle. He thinks I should kill as many as I want because they probably have diseases anyway. I don't know if I can trust Chet regarding animal sensitivity. He's a member of PITA (People for Intensive Testing on Animals).

Mair, you have been very helpful regarding content in my book which may be misinterpreted by advocacy groups and others with too much time on their hands. Do you think killing more monkeys will upset animal lovers?

Thanks,

Grady

- - - - - - - - - - - - - - - - - - -

To: Grady Thoms
From: Mair Pearson
Re: Animal Cruelty in Fiction

Grady, I think animal rights activists are more concerned with actual animals, not the ones in your head. The only way they might object is if your work of fiction encourages or promotes animal abuse. I do not believe it does.

Mair

- - - - - - - - - - - - - - - - - - -

To: Mair Pearson
Cc: Bill Williams
From: Grady Thoms
Subject: Grady Thoms Is Off the Market

Mair, you might be interested to know that Jenny and I are pretty much official as of 7:45 p.m. last night. After the BRAG writing group met (we have six members now), Jenny and I went for a walk. Sometimes we like to stroll up the hill to the wealthy neighborhoods and point out our favorite foreclosed homes. There's a house I like with a giant Douglas fir in the front yard. Unfortunately, the previous owners spray-painted "Chase Bank can suck it" on the garage door.

As the sun was setting, Jenny asked if I planned to kiss her anytime soon. My stomach knotted up. For once, I had nothing to say. After an awkward minute of fidgeting with my clothes, I asked her how Tuesday sounded. She said we should never put off tomorrow what can be accomplished today. I was about to tell her that really only applies to chores and work-related projects when she pulled me in and kissed me right on the lips. Can you believe it? At that moment, it started to drizzle. It was as if God created a moment so beautiful between two people that the angels started to cry. I got dizzy and had to sit down.

Now that Jenny and I are exclusive, I should probably close down my accounts on Monster Match and SingleMeat.com. I really hope it works out between us. In past relationships, I've made mistakes I hope to never repeat, like writing the wrong girl's name on a homemade back rub coupon. As it turns out, women don't like being confused with other women on back rub coupons (also, don't put an expiration date on it).

I know this has nothing to do with my book, but I feel like you and Bill have shared all aspects of my life the last six months. Our friendship is not only about *Mr. Nary.*

Thanks,

Grady

- - - - - - - - - - - - - - - - - -

To: Grady Thoms
Cc: Bill Williams
From: Mair Pearson
Subject: Grady Thoms Is Off the Market

Grady, as I have told you before, many of us here have become intrigued with your pilgrimage toward authorship. In fact, I receive daily requests from several colleagues asking to forward any recent correspondence from you. I am sure they will enjoy reading about you "making angels cry."
Mair

- - - - - - - - - - - - - - - - - -

To: Mair Pearson
Cc: Bill Williams
From: Grady Thoms

Mair, the attempt to rescue Alegria failed. A Brazilian guard jumped on her back while she was trying to board one of the Piranha Assault boats. She falls into the water and drowns. If it's any consolation, the sexy guard drowns too. Haha! Just kidding, Alegria does not die. In good conscious, I could not kill her. The love she and Pubano share is just too strong. Even the author could not break it. However, she does become paralyzed from the waist down.

Chuck Nary and Pubano were smart to attack Hector Raul's mansion in broad daylight. While the Bolivian navy occupied the shapely guards and spider monkeys, Pubano and Nary snuck into the mansion to save Alegria. Chuck Nary, who was suffering from the shakes of no booze, still has a large bounty on his head. Hector Raul promised $20,000 and a gift certificate to *Victoria's El Secreto* to any guard who kills him.

Once in the palace, Nary and Pubano separate. Pubano finds Alegria in a dank room in the basement, where they embrace for several minutes. Alegria, fearing the worst, asks Pubano how she looks. Knowing his vain wife would ask, Pubano does the wise thing and lies, saying he prefers her without makeup anyway.

From the balcony of his master bedroom, Hector Raul spots the intruders and triggers the emergency shutdown, which locks down the mansion and releases the spider monkeys. As you can imagine, an incredible fight wages on the veranda between the foxy guards, the spider monkeys, and the Bolivian navy.

The fight between Chuck Nary and Hector Raul is abrupt. Nary finds him on the balcony where they exchange a few words. Nary tells him he will *pay for Pey.* Hector responds by saying Nary is a stupid gringo who should have never come to Bolivia. Hector charges at Nary. As he takes a swing, Nary crouches down, wraps him around his knees, and flings him over his shoulder off the balcony. The drug lord lands on the stone patio below, his body lies in a contorted position, but he is not quite dead. A few spider moneys, rabid from being fed the Naga Viper peppers Nary left outside their tree houses, attack Hector to death.

I let Chet read this entry, and he says it reeks of laziness. He claims it is anticlimactic. He may be right. Chet is not a bad writer himself. As you know, his Yelp reviews are legendary and feared by local businesses. With 322 followers, one bad review from Chet can mean bankruptcy. He once wrote a scathing review for Gracie's Candles, a local store with candles made by volunteers from the Brookstone Retirement Community. They had to close shop a couple weeks after Chet's review because he simply wrote, "Gracie's candles are as uninspired as the hands that made them." You can see why I can't get on his bad side. I may need to rewrite this.

Chet did like the part about Alegria getting hit in the thigh with a poisoned dart while they were trying to escape. This is why she is paralyzed from the waist down. I figure this will upset some readers, especially the women, but at this point they have learned to expect the unexpected. Besides, Alegria will still be able to work at the bakery.

Thanks,

Grady

- - - - - - - - - - - - - - - - - - -

To: Grady Thoms
From: Mair Pearson
Re: THE Battle Conclusion

Grady, you will have to do many edits and rewrites, but only when your manuscript is completed. This is just the first draft. Do not worry about changes now (as you will learn, the real work begins after you have written the novel).

It may be important to receive feedback from others, but remember you are the author with the vision. You feel the tone of the story. It will ruin your writing life if you seek compliments.

Mair

- - - - - - - - - - - - - - - - - - -

To: Mair Pearson
Cc: Bill Williams
From: Grady Thoms
Subject: The Twist

Mair, I have moved on from THE Battle and plan to add one final twist. Bill's book had a couple nice little twists like that one guy who was not who he said he was and that other guy who did something unexpected. I think I'll do a twist like that but go totally bigger and better.

One idea I'm pondering is that the death of Hector Raul has unexpected global consequences. As it turns out, Hector Raul was also a Chilean ambassador of goodwill, and his death sparks outrage in Chile. Since the Bolivian navy was directly involved in the assassination, the Chilean government immediately imposes sanctions against their neighbors. Tensions reach an all-time high as both countries begin lining the mountainous border with troops. War is imminent.

Chuck Nary decides this is not his fight and heads for the airport. With Hector Raul dead and no missing couple to find, he decides it's a good time to leave. He has business left in the United States—to find the woman who set him up. Unfortunately, Pubano is called into service and the two friends must part.

I don't think I'll describe too much of the impending war between Bolivia and Chile. I'll just let the reader know that a conflict is well underway as Nary's plane lifts off.

Maybe later Chuck Nary will be watching the news and see Bolivia has lost the war. The skirmish cost a few thousand lives, crippled their economy, and the landlocked country loses even more of its land to Chile. I would have liked Bolivia to win the war, but I just don't see it happening. Chile's military is way more advanced. You can look it up. I have to keep the integrity of my novel intact.

Thanks,

Grady

- - - - - - - - - - - - - - - - - - -

To: Grady Thoms
From: Mair Pearson
Re: The Twist

Grady, let me get this straight. Your novel, *Mr. Nary*, is about a private eye who travels to Bolivia, causes an indefinite amount of damage during fights and car chases, ruins an annual celebration, and becomes a drunk who abuses animals. Many innocent people die, including a poor orphan and a gentleman by the name of Chester Biggles. Furthermore, an innocent women is kidnapped and becomes paralyzed from the waist down in a botched rescue attempt.

To top it off, the protagonist sparks an international conflict leading to mass death and leaves Bolivia in economic crisis. This is the basic story of your novel, am I correct? I just want to be clear here.
Mair

- - - - - - - - - - - - - - - - - - -

To: Mair Pearson
From: Grady Thoms
Re: The Twist

Mair, when you put it that way, you make it sound as if Chuck Nary should have never gone to Bolivia in the first place.
Thanks,
Grady

- - - - - - - - - - - - - - - - - - -

To: Mair Pearson
Cc: Bill Williams
From: Grady Thoms
Subject: Cover Art

Mair, with just a couple chapters to go, it's time to start thinking about the cover. It needs to have elements of foreign danger, forbidden romance, and exotic intrigue.

Let's do a collage-style painting that is tasteful yet intense. For the backdrop, we should use the skyline of La Paz tucked between a few peaks of the Andes Mountains. On one side of the cover, Chuck Nary is running away from an exploding bus while carrying a baby and a briefcase. Even though there is not a scene like this in the book, it gives the reader an idea of the kind of stuff that does happen. If anyone complains, we can just say it was in the book but you decided to edit it out. Chuck Nary's character should look like a young Steve McQueen with a mustache. That will solve my problem of trying to write in his mustache in the beginning of the book.

On the other side of the book, we should have the drug lord Senor Hector Raul. He's holding a bag of cocaine and a grenade. There's a cigarette dangling from his lips. His eyes are dark and cold. Behind Raul's left shoulder, off in the distance, a woman will stand in the shadows wearing a trench coat and sunglasses. This will represent Sophia, the one who deceived Nary. She should have long, tan legs. The trench coat will come down to about midthigh. To avoid offending anyone, we can include a little excerpt on the inside sleeve stating the woman on the front cover is wearing shorts and a T-shirt underneath the trench coat.

On the bottom of the book, a small, squatty native, Pubano, will be shooting a pistol into the air. He should look a little like Herve Villechaize from *Fantasy Island,* but taller. Pey will be next to him, doing a karate kick into the air.

If we have room, we should include a few other items in the collage. You can pick three or four of the following: a jeep driving on a mountainous pass, a helicopter, a vial of poison, sticks of dynamite strapped to a llama, a bull charging people at an open market, and a street orphan looking up poignantly at an Incan statue. There should be a lot of rich reds, bright oranges, and deep greens throughout the cover.

It would be great if someone in your department could start working on this. For optimal results, make five prototypes and I'll pick the best one. Thanks,
Grady

- - - - - - - - - - - - - - - - - - -

To: Grady Thoms
From: Mair Pearson
Re: Cover Art

Grady, this will be no problem at all. How would you like to pay for the designer…check, cash, or credit card? We outsource cover design work, so five cover mockups will come to roughly three grand, but I may be able to get you a special deal from a cartoonist I know.
Mair

To: Mair Pearson
From: Grady Thoms
Re: Cover Art

Mair, why does it cost so much? Is it the exploding bus? What if we only do two prototypes and we take out Pubano, the woman in the trench coat, and the bull? Let's just have Chuck Nary and Senor Hector with the skyline of La Paz on the cover. Forget everything else.

Maybe the designer could include one helicopter in the sky. How hard is it to draw a helicopter? Have him just cut one out from a magazine and trace over it.

Thanks,

Grady

- - - - - - - - - - - - - - - - - - - -

To: Grady Thoms
From: Mair Pearson
Re: Cover Art

Grady, the cover design should be the farthest thing from your mind right now. Publishers reserve the right to choose the title and design the cover, so you should concentrate on finishing the novel.

If you must know, much of the cost of original artwork will come from hiring models for Chuck Nary and Hector Raul on the cover.

Mair

- - - - - - - - - - - - - - - - - - - -

To: Mair Pearson
From: Grady Thoms
Re: Cover Art

Okay Mair, let's just do one prototype and let's not have any people on the cover. I don't have a lot of money to spend on this. Instead, we could do the Andes Mountains, a helicopter, and a llama. How much are we looking at now?

Thanks, Grady

To: Grady Thoms
From: Mair Pearson
Re: Cover Art

Grady, if you only have a llama on the cover, people might think this is a book about a llama whose name is Mr. Nary. Again, forget about the cover and finish writing the book.
Mair

To: Mair Pearson
From: Grady Thoms
Re: Cover Art

Mair, I do want Chuck Nary on the cover, but I can't afford it. I see your point about people mistaking the llama as Mr. Nary. What if we add a subtitle to the book? The book could be called *Mister Nary: The Story of a Man.* That way, we could keep the llama on the cover and people will know this is a book about a man. I included a detailed drawing.
Thanks,
Grady

To: Grady Thoms
From: Mair Pearson
Re: Cover Art

Grady, your drawing of the cover may just make it in the book. I made copies of it and handed them out in the office. Some have posted it on their cubical walls.

I spoke with Bill, and he has agreed to pay for the design of the cover as well as other costs on one condition—you allow us to publish this as *The Story of How Grady Thoms Got Published.* We would publish the correspondence rather than the *Mr. Nary* novel.

Bill and I think your journey to becoming a published author is more interesting than the novel you created. Bill says there is a strong market for humor, as well as how-to books, and you could be a significant contribution to this genre.
Mair

- - - - - - - - - - - - - - - - - - -

To: Mair Pearson
From: Grady Thoms
Re: Cover Art

Mair, you're being sarcastic, right? I am relieved to hear that Bill will pay for the cost of the cover. This is great news. However, I have no interest in publishing our correspondence. That seems crazy. *Mr. Nary* is the novel we should publish. It's almost done. Let's revive the ideas I mentioned above. How long will it take to have the prototypes for me to review?
Thanks,
Grady

- - - - - - - - - - - - - - - - - - -

To: Grady Thoms
From: Mair Pearson
Re: Cover Art

Grady, we are serious. Finish the book, and we'll discuss what actually gets published later.
Mair

- - - - - - - - - - - - - - - - - - -

To: Mair Pearson
Cc: Bill Williams
From: Grady Thoms
Subject: Nary Returns to the United States

Mair, the book is wrapping up. It has not been easy to focus and finish these last couple chapters. Luckily, Chet had some Ritalin leftover from when he was misdiagnosed with ADHD (Attention Deficit H-something Disorder). I tried to take the quiz online to see if I have Attention Deficit Disorder but got distracted and started watching plane crashes on YouTube.

Chet says to crush a Ritalin into a cup of espresso and I'll finish my book in no time. He calls it a Danish coffee. Chet might be right. I've already completed the first page of the last chapter.

> *Chuck Nary, tired of being on the run and having the runs, was relieved to be back in Texas. He missed people with one-syllable names like Dave, Jim, Al, Paps, Gary, and Slim.*
>
> *Checking his phone, Nary saw he had nine messages. Most were from lonely women looking for a steak dinner, some lovin', or both. One voice mail, however, caught his attention. It was Sophia.*
>
> *Trying to sound calm, Sophia was checking in, wondering if Mr. Nary had any leads on the missing couple from the cruise ship. The message, left five days ago, was clearly a test to see if he was still alive. Sophia had not heard from Mr. Nary or any of the assassins for a while. Surely she is anxious to know what happened in Bolivia.*
>
> *Nary hatched a plan. Using his best French/Canadian accent, he would call Sophia as Clyde and tell her he had completed the job. Maybe she would ask to meet. She might want proof of Chuck Nary's death. Clyde would have demanded payment. A meeting would be natural.*

Walking out of the Houston airport, Nary waved down a cab and bypassed the line of people who were waiting in the taxi line. He was in a hurry. Ignoring their angry shouts, Nary slid into the cab and began rehearsing what he would say to the wench.

I think this is enough writing for today. Jenny and I are going to take Chet out to a movie. He is feeling down today. I guess he googled his name to see who he shares it with and found another Chet Jensen in Maine who photographs cats wearing top hats and monocles.

I'll let you know when the book is completed. It should be just a couple more days.

Thanks,

Grady

- - - - - - - - - - - - - - - - - - -

To: Mair Pearson
Cc: Bill Williams
From: Grady Thoms
Subject: Sophia Goes to Jail

Mair, Chuck Nary gave Sophia a taste of her own dirty medicine. Thinking she is meeting Clyde at the hotel bar of the Embassy Suites, Sophia walks into the lobby only to see Nary with a couple cops. She drops her purse in shock. As she is handcuffed, she spits in Mr. Nary's face.

Do you think it will be okay if Mr. Nary slaps her across the face before the police take her away? After all, she did set him up and nearly killed him several times. And she did spit in his face, so it is sort of justified. Is a slap justified or are you one of those people who think a woman should never be punched under any circumstances?

Chet thinks after Sophia spits in his face, Mr. Nary should give her a long smooch instead. That does sound like something Mr. Nary would do.

Thanks,

Grady

- - - - - - - - - - - - - - - - - - -

To: Grady Thoms
From: Mair Pearson
Re: Sophia Goes to Jail

Grady, I tend to fall in that small but proud category that believes it is never okay to hit a woman. I will even go so far as to say you should not strike children, the elderly, the unprovoked, or anyone else outside of a boxing ring.

I really do not wish to impede the content of your book, but I would like to see Chuck Nary take the high road here. If Sophia spits in his face, maybe Nary could use one of his patent zingers before she is hauled away.
Mair

- - - - - - - - - - - - - - - - - - -

To: Mair Pearson
From: Grady Thoms
Re: Sofia Goes to Jail

Mair, thanks for the advice. I've decided to use a combination of the ideas from you and Chet. After Sophia spits in Nary's face, he pulls her in for a passionate kiss and says *that's all the man you'll be tasting for the next twenty to twenty-five years. You're welcome.*

I think this is a satisfactory conclusion to Sophia. Now all the loose ends are tied up. There are just a couple more pages to write and I am done.
Thanks,
Grady

- - - - - - - - - - - - - - - - - - -

To: Grady Thoms
From: Mair Pearson
Re: Sophia Goes to Jail

Grady, I knew you had it in you. Congratulations on finishing the first draft of your novel. This has been quite the experience, to say the least.
Mair

To: Mair Pearson
Cc: Bill Williams
From: Grady Thoms
Subject: Closing Paragraph

Mair and Bill, I'm nearly done with *Mister Nary.* I feel a little emotional about it and hope to end the book in a profound way. In the end, Chuck Nary is with his dad, Robert Nary, and they're sitting on a dock staring out at Galveston Bay while smoking cigars, drinking whiskey, and watching fireworks. I want it to end with some advice from the elder Nary. I have a couple options:

Robert Nary took a sip of his 62 Dalmore single-malt scotch and cleared his throat.

"You know son," he said as the colors exploded above them, "freedom is doing what you want, but doing what you want can cost you your freedom."

The younger Nary nodded and gazed into the horizon. He had never heard truer words.

Or this:

As *the sounds of thunder shook above their heads, Robert Nary removed his cowboy hat and put his arm around his son.*

"You know, Chuck," he began, "when you're a young man, you count your drinks and your women. Later on, you count your money." He paused to gnaw on his Cohiba cigar. "Toward the end of life, you're just countin' your days."

Chuck Nary looked over the bay and thought about what his dad said. They may have been the truest words ever spoken.

THE END

What do you think? I wrote this with tears in my eyes. The book is done. I am proud.

Thanks,

Grady

To: Grady Thoms
Cc: Mair Pearson
From: Bill Williams
Re: Closing Paragraph

Grady, both of these paragraphs are solid endings for Mr. Nary. Everyone at the office was very eager to know how it was going to end. We voted seven to four to go with the second one (the one with the elder Nary counting stuff).

I think we have what we need to get going on How Grady Thoms Got Published. I will try to get a contract in the mail to you this week. This may have a chance to sell.

Regards,
Bill

- - - - - - - - - - - - - - - - - - -

To: Bill Williams
Cc: Mair Pearson
From: Grady Thoms
Re: Closing Paragraph

Bill, your e-mail was confusing. Are you really planning to publish my e-mails and not the book? Are you messing with me? I don't think I will allow you to poke fun of my inexperience at my expense. It may be funny in your staff meetings, but it's not very funny to me.

Let's get something straight. I write thriller fiction, not humor. You haven't even seen the final manuscript yet. I will not allow you to belittle *Mr. Nary* by publishing my private e-mails with you and Mair and passing it off as humor. I guess I will start looking for a new publisher, one who will take *Mr. Nary* seriously.

Thanks,
Grady

- - - - - - - - - - - - - - - - - - -

To: Grady Thoms
Cc: Mair Pearson
From: Bill Williams
Subject: Closing Paragraph

Grady, attached is an author contract for *The Story of How Grady Thoms Got Published.* We can discuss publishing your novel down the road if this first book takes off like I think it can. It includes a $5,000 cash advance and 15 percent royalties on all books sold.
Regards,
Bill

- - - - - - - - - - - - - - - - - - -

To: Bill Williams
Cc: Mair Pearson
From: Grady Thoms
Re: Closing Paragraph

Bill, after much deliberation, I have decided to let you publish our correspondence. The decision was not easy. I want you to know I am not doing it for the money. This book will be for all the aspiring authors out there. I will sacrifice a little dignity and pride to give hope to millions of young writers. Again, it is *not* about making a quick buck.

I have one final request before I sign the contract—bump the royalties to 20 percent and you got a deal.
Thanks.
Grady

- - - - - - - - - - - - - - - - - - -

To: Grady Thoms
Cc: Mair Pearson
From: Bill Williams
Re: Closing Paragraph

Okay Grady, 20 percent it is. Only because I know it's not about the money. You make me laugh.

Bill

One Year Later

To: Grady Thoms
From: Bill Williams
Subject: Update

Grady, I hope this e-mail finds you well. As you may have realized, *The Story of How Grady Thoms Got Published* is not a New York Times best seller. However, it is developing a cult following among the youth. A representative from Powell's Books in Portland said it has become very popular with the unemployed and postgraduate hipsters. They have requested fifty more copies. They are filing *Mr. Nary* in the "Irony" section. Whatever that means.

You should know that Mair no longer works for me. She moved back to Colorado to be closer to her family. I know she will never forget working with you.

I mailed you a check for current royalties. It's not much, but it should cover expenses while you work on the next book. Maybe you can write that wilderness guide for women lost in the woods? Your unique audience might like that.

Let me know if you change addresses. A few more checks will be on the way here and there. You can now officially call yourself an author. Congratulations.

Regards,

Bill

- - - - - - - - - - - - - - - - - - -

To: Bill Williams
From: Grady Thoms
Re: Update

Thanks Bill, I will always be indebted to you and Mair. I never knew she was from Colorado. Now that I think about it, I didn't know much about her at all. Most of our correspondence was about me. I guess you never know how selfish you are until you start thinking about others.

I'm glad this book found an audience. I never have viewed myself as funny, but if that is what people want, I guess I'm happy to oblige. I owe it all to you and Mair. If you talk to her, thank her for me.

As far as me working on a second book, I think I'll pass. It was not at all what I expected. Mair was right about the editing and rewriting. It is downright exhausting. Rereading the novel over and over again has brought up painful memories. I never knew a guy like Chuck Nary could not only ruin a novel, but could nearly ruin my life. Besides, knowing my books are "ironic" has probably ruined the irony now.

Thanks for the checks. They were needed. I plan to buy a guitar and pursue a new passion. Chet and I are going to start a band. Jenny will play the tambourine and sing backup vocals. I'll be lead vocals, as well as head songwriter. It should be a lot easier than writing a book.

Look for us on MTV.

Thanks,

Grady

CPSIA information can be obtained at www.ICGtesting.com
Printed in the USA
LVOW06s2023290414

383731LV00003B/187/P